As a Burning Flame

The Dream of Regina Jonas

Written and illustrated by

Noa Mishkin

somewhere

An imprint of Ayin Press

Brooklyn, New York

As a Burning Flame: The Dream of Regina Jonas

Written and illustrated by Noa Mishkin

Originally created as a final project in the Visual Communications department
at Bezalel Academy of Art and Design, Jerusalem, June 2022
Advisor: Amit Trainin

This book was made possible through the generous support of the Opaline Fund and
Anne Germanacos / Firehouse Fund. We are grateful for their commitment to the
transformative power of creative work, and to amplifying a polyphony of voices from
within and beyond the Jewish world.

ISBN (paperback): 979-8-9867803-2-0
ISBN (hardcover): 978-1-961814-19-6
ISBN (e-book): 979-8-9867803-5-1

Library of Congress Control Number: 2023940371

Cover and interior design by Noa Mishkin
Layout and typesetting by Cory Rockliff

First edition
First printing
Printed and bound in the USA

Published by Somewhere, an imprint of Ayin Press
Brooklyn, New York

www.somewherebooks.com
www.ayinpress.org

Distributed by Publishers Group West, an Ingram Brand

Somewhere books may be purchased at a discounted rate by book clubs, community
organizations, synagogues, and other institutions buying in bulk.
For more information, please email info@ayinpress.org.

Follow @AyinPress on Facebook, Instagram, or Twitter and
@SomewhereBooks on Instagram.

To Noam,
Mommy and Abba

I have been religious since I was born, and a feminist since around age fifteen. But I'd heard Regina Jonas's name for the first time only in 2021. She wasn't in the canon of "Trailblazing Jewish Women" I had grown up with, nor was she a fixture on the usual list of "Religious Leaders of the Holocaust."

Regina Jonas was the first Ashkenazi woman to be ordained as a rabbi, and while I was raised in a world where there were many learned women, no one knew what to call them—Rebbetzin? Rabba? Rabbi?

I came to Regina's story already knowing who I was, after I had allowed myself to search for the Jewish life that suited me outside the confines of my Modern Orthodox upbringing. And still, when I first encountered them, Regina's words were incredibly comforting and affirming to me. Almost one hundred years separate us, but her voice pierces my heart as though she were standing next to me, reminding me that I am on the right path.

The first time I heard anyone call a woman "Rabbi," I was twenty-one.

It's not that I wasn't raised in liberal religious institutions—I definitely was.

I grew up in a Modern Orthodox American-Israeli family. I attended a religious elementary school and an all-girls high school, and after graduating, I studied at a seminary before my army service. In the years that followed, I studied in yet another women's beit midrash.

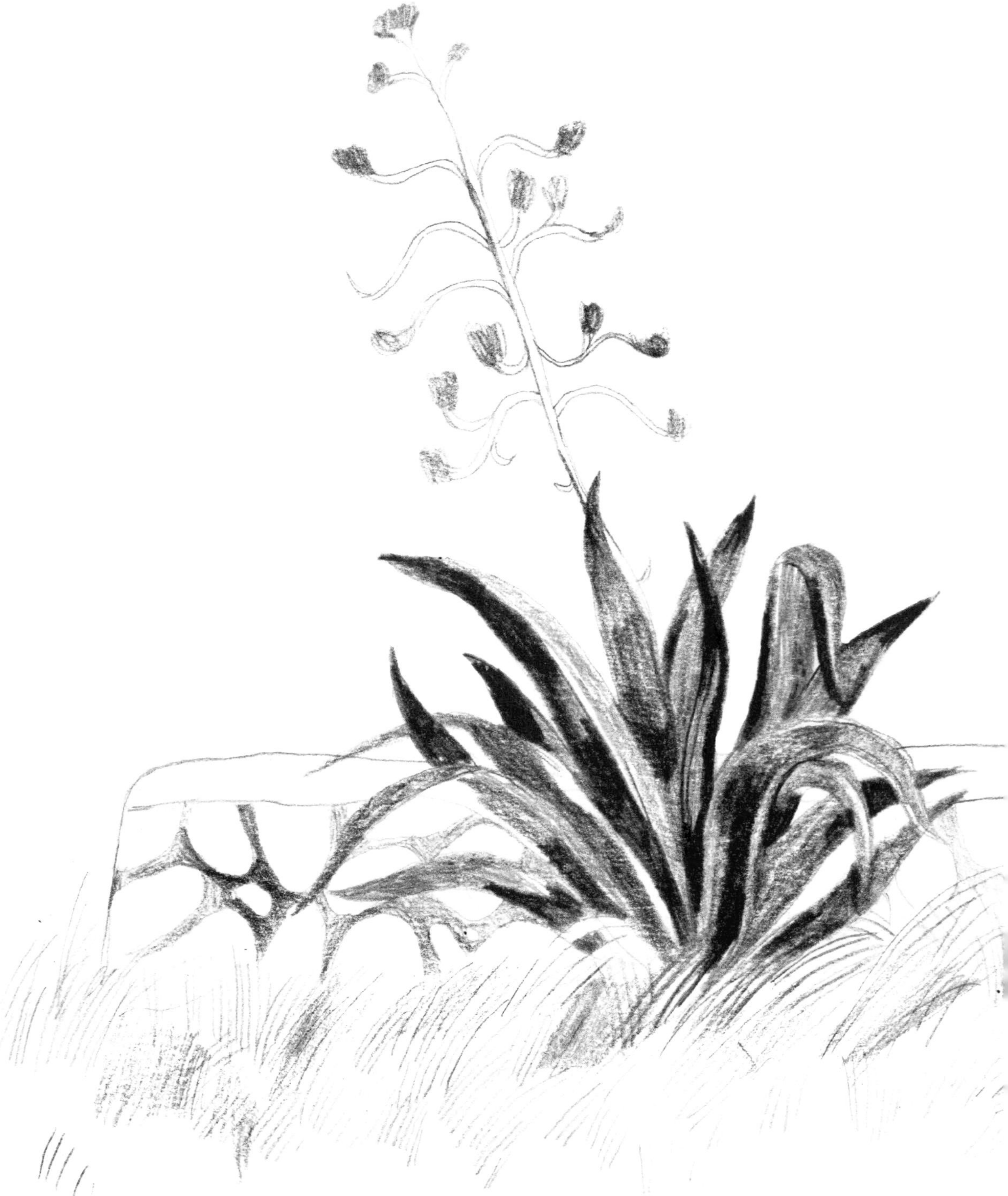

There was no shortage of female teachers alongside the rabbis in all these places. I studied Talmud, and shook the lulav, and participated in endless debates about feminism and halacha (Jewish law). And it always came back to the same conclusion: Judaism is capable of progress, and can become more egalitarian, but only up to a certain point. *In the end,* my teachers and parents explained, *women are women and men are men. A woman cannot be counted in a minyan, or testify in a beit din, or read from the Torah. That's the halacha. That's just how it is.*

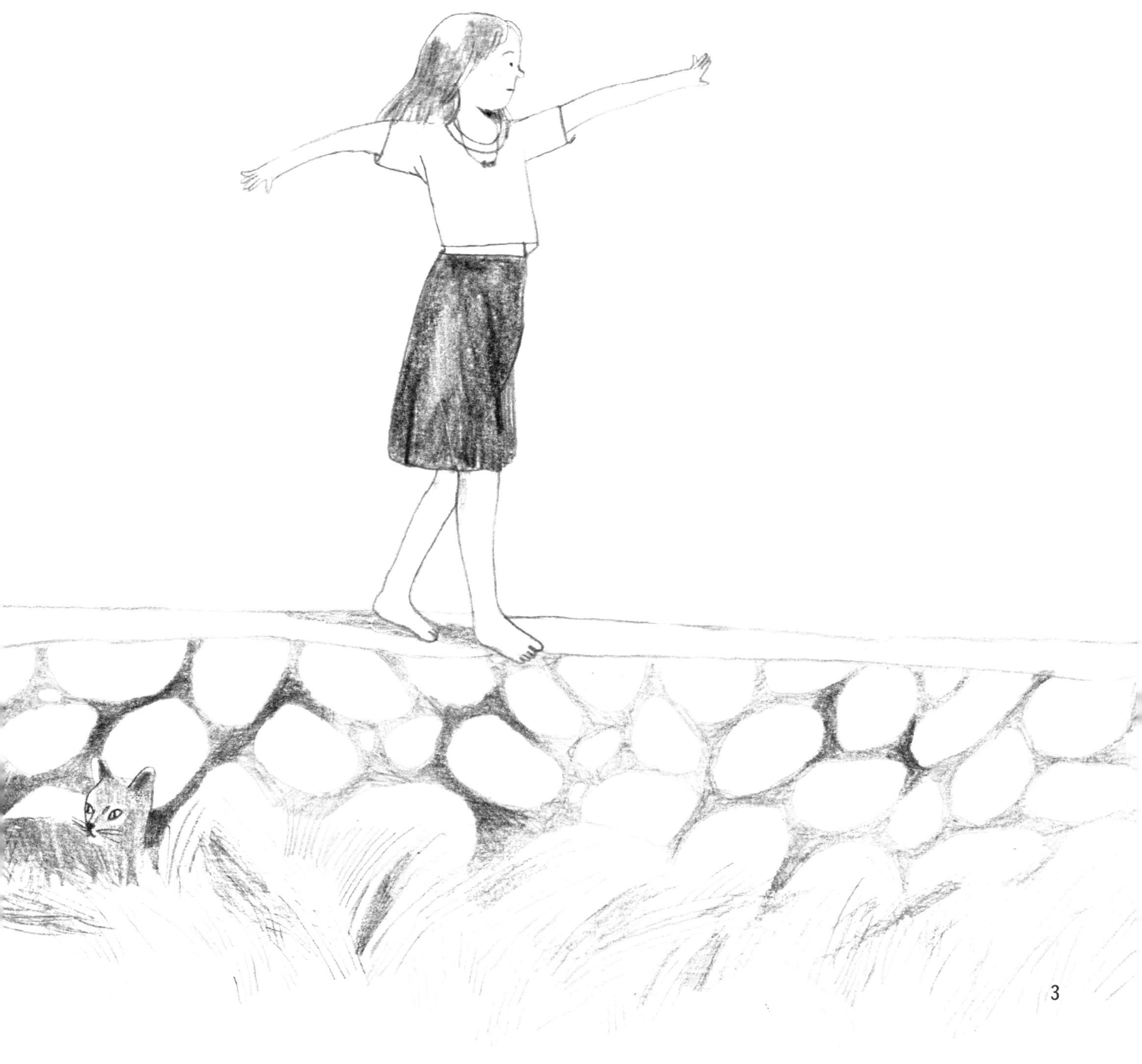

With Righteousness and Justice

1922–1935

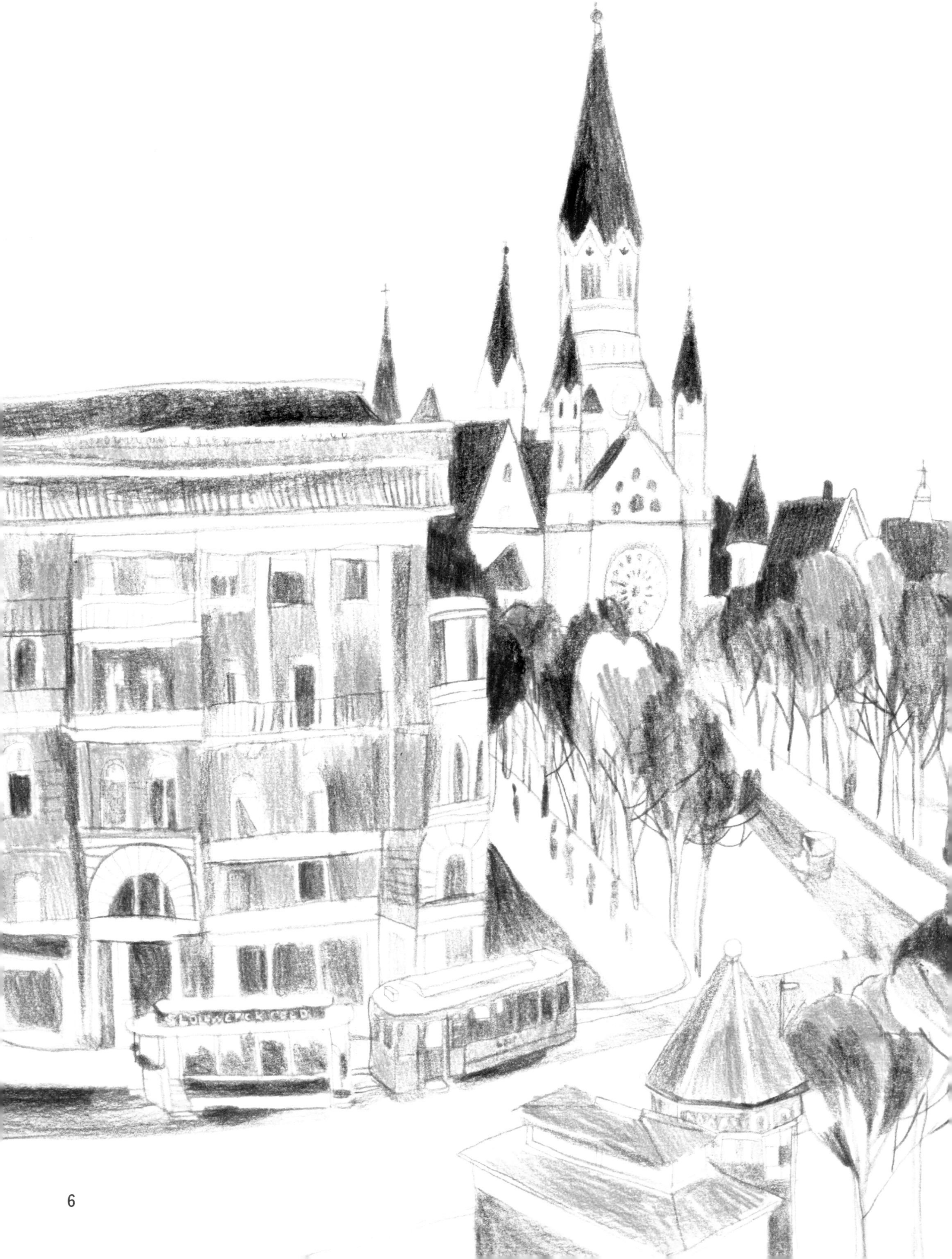

Regina Jonas was born in 1902 to a poor, religious family in Berlin. At age twenty-two, she began studying at the Higher Institute for Jewish Studies, a rabbinical seminary that ordained* rabbis and trained teachers of religious studies.

Women who studied at the seminary were certified as an "Academic Teacher of Religion" at their graduation, but they were not eligible for rabbinical semikha like their male counterparts. Regina not only petitioned to be ordained, but in 1930, she presented her case for women's rabbinical ordination in her master's thesis, "Can a Woman Hold Rabbinic Office?" In it, she argued for the halachic permissibility and right of women to perform the duties of modern rabbis.

* Semikha, or rabbinical ordination, is the granting of authority to rule on halachic matters (to pasken) and the right to be called "Rabbi." Semikha can be granted only by an existing rabbi who himself was ordained by a previously licensed rabbi, and so on. According to tradition, this chain continues all the way back to Moses.

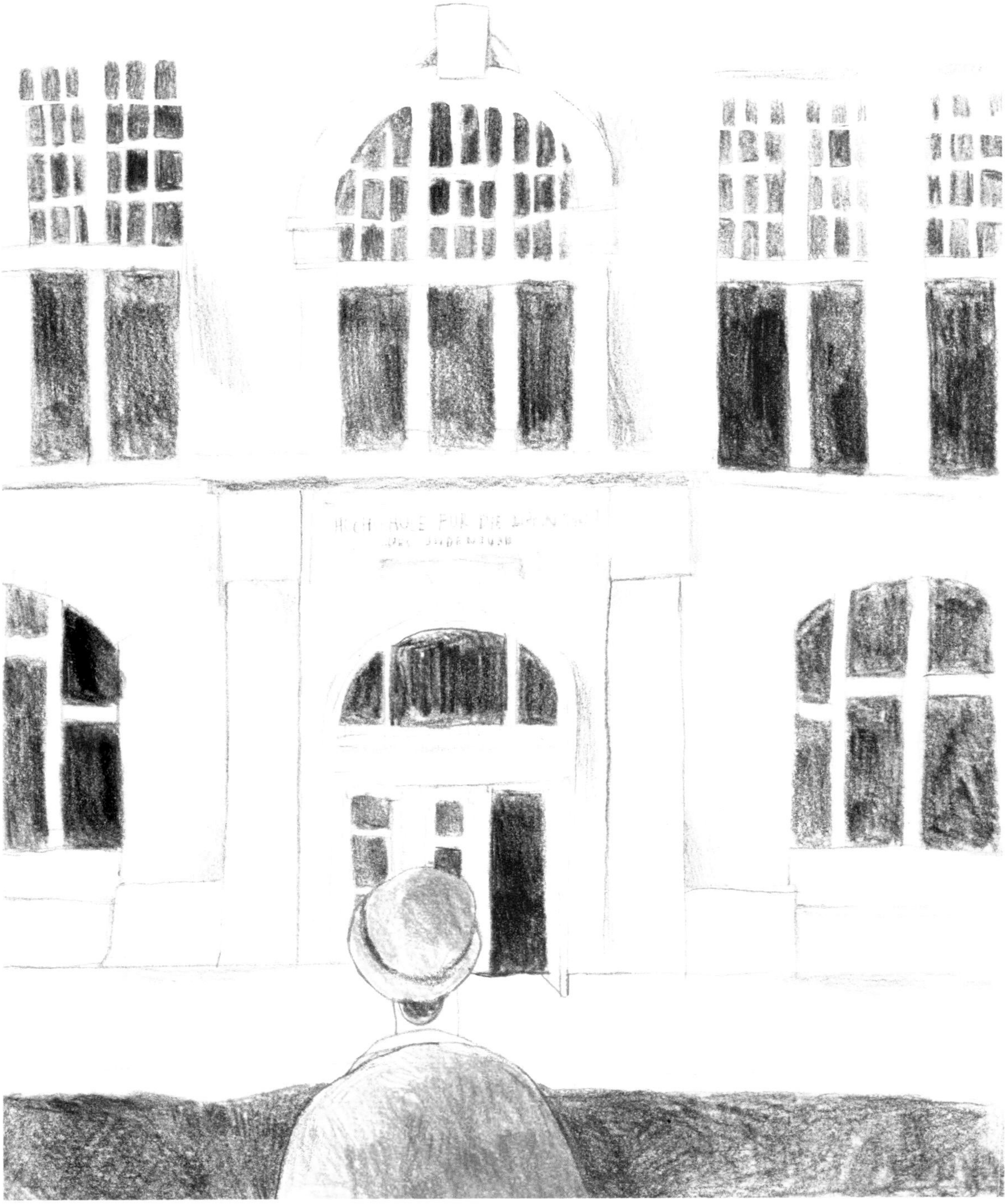

In her thesis, Regina stated: **« I believe that the question of whether a woman may make halachic decisions as a rabbinerin* may very clearly be seen as permitted, and it is not necessary to continue to linger over this matter. . . . Just as both female doctors and teachers in time have become a necessity from a psychological standpoint, so has the female rabbi. »**

* Rabbinerin is the feminine form of "rabbi" (rabbiner) in German and was generally used as a title for rabbis' wives, much like rebbetzin (in Yiddish) or rabbanit (in Hebrew).

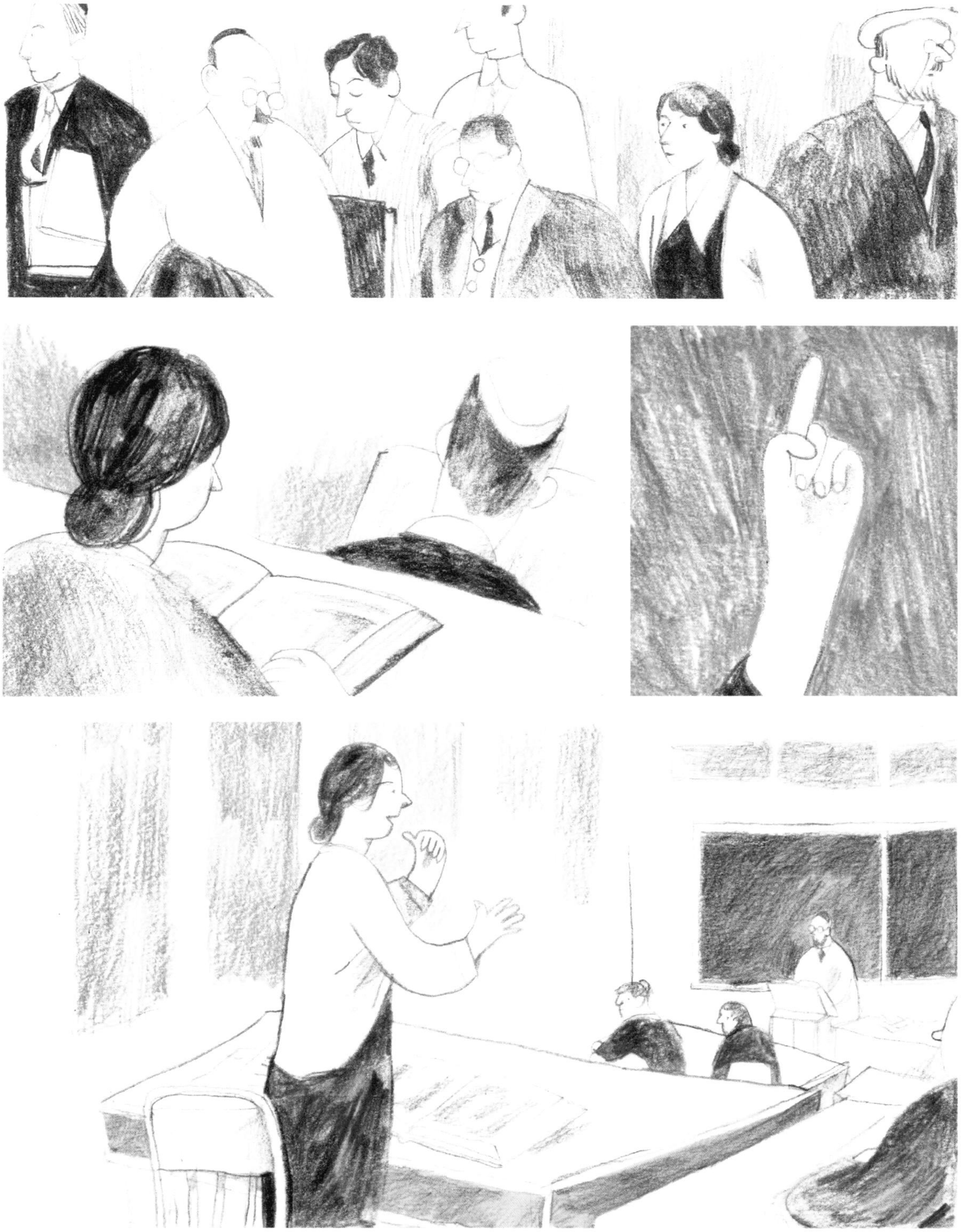

« There are even some things that women can say to youth, which cannot be said by the man in the pulpit. Her experiences, her psychological observations, are profoundly different from those of a man, therefore she has a different style. »

[*Can a Woman Hold Rabbinic Office?,* June 1930]

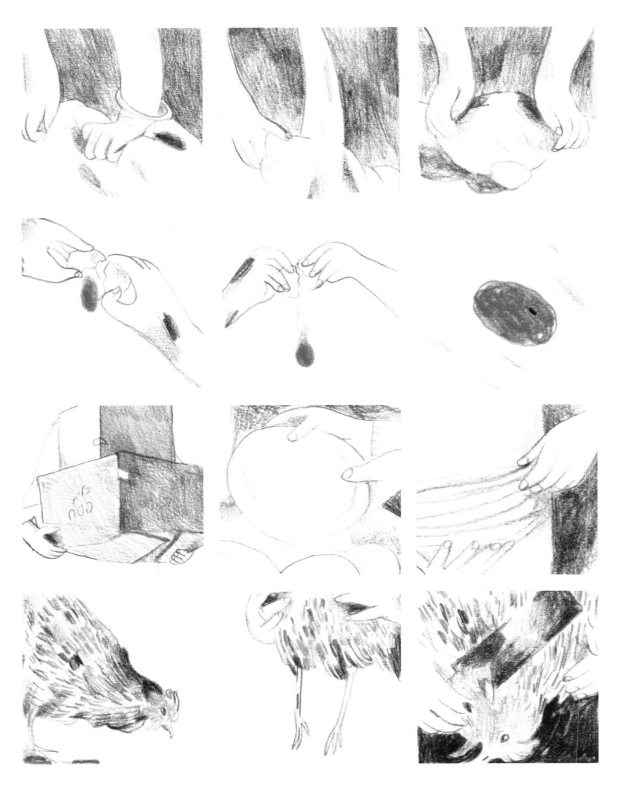

Women have always had halachic authority, Regina argued, as they are the managers of the kosher home, and make legal decisions daily, when no man or rabbi is present: « Their entire work as household 'supervisor' is [in effect] to pasken. This is possible for, in this area, she knows something: no one else can represent her and therefore she has

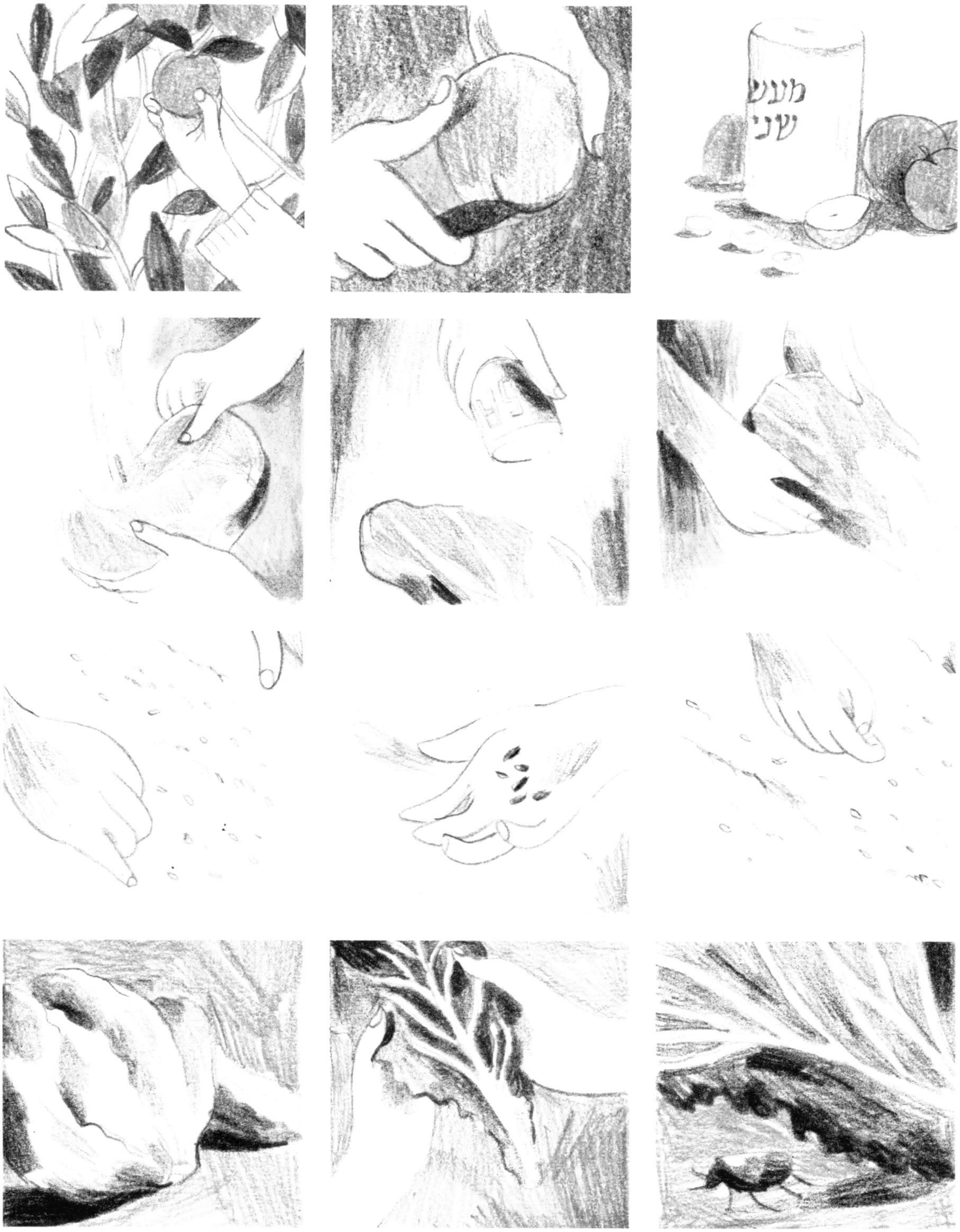
מעש
שני

the chance to demonstrate in practice that she can summon the requisite understanding and seriousness for such matters. If she now has a career as a rabbi and must make decisions in other areas in which she has studied, then nothing revolutionary has happened. » [*Can a Woman Hold Rabbinic Office?*, June 1930]

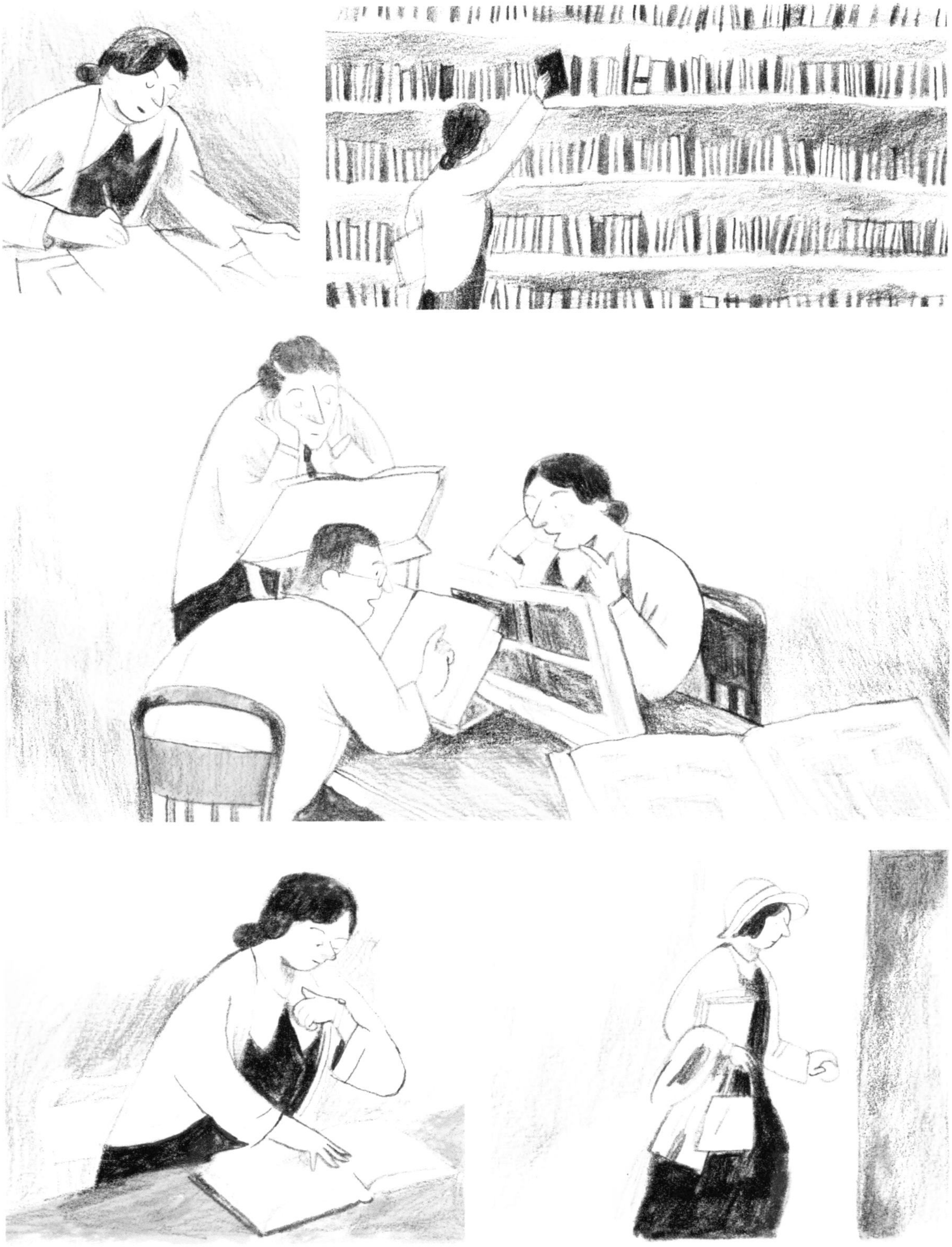

The logical conclusion was clear: « **Other than prejudice and unfamiliarity, almost nothing opposes a woman holding the rabbinical office halachically.** »

[*Can a Woman Hold Rabbinic Office?*, June 1930]

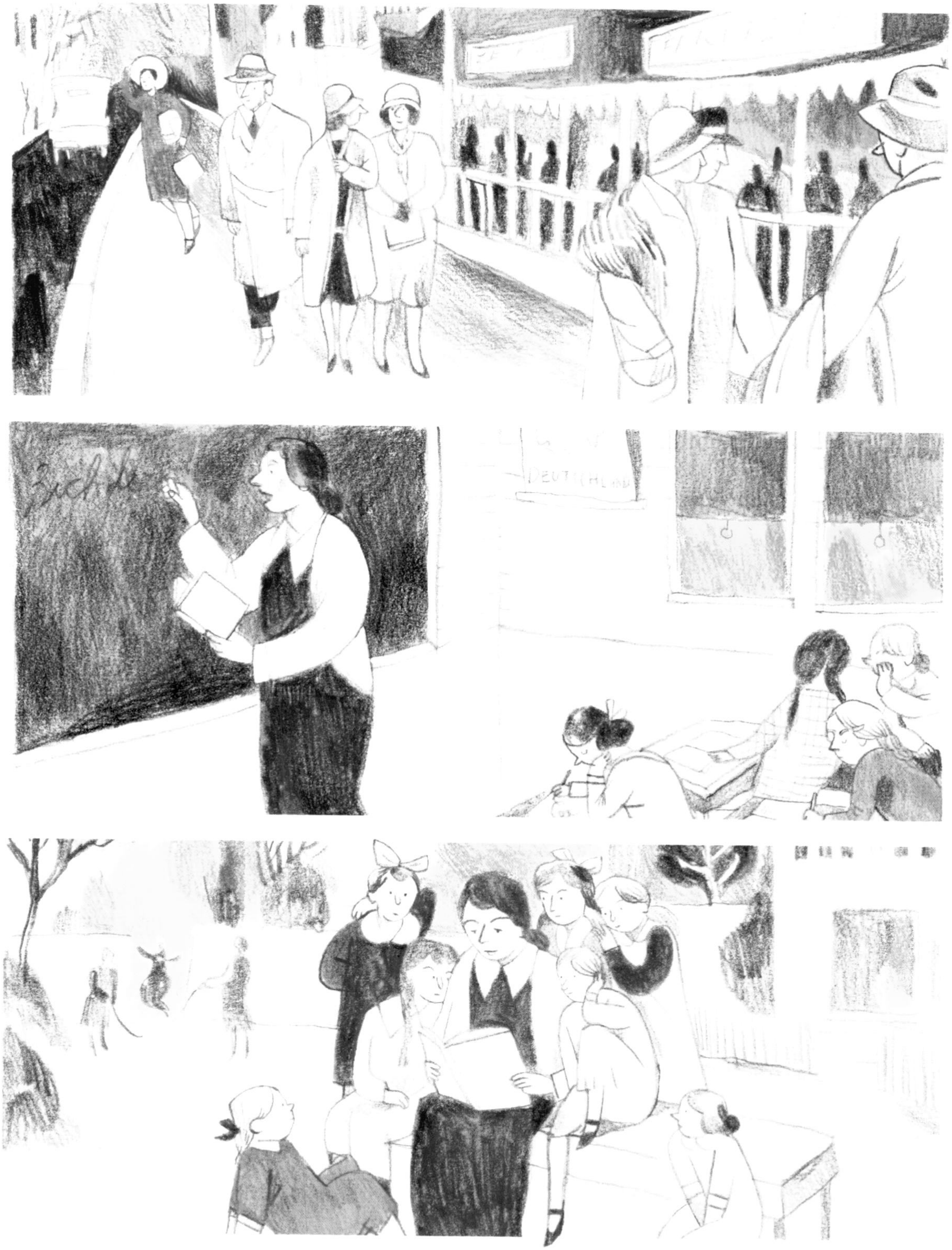

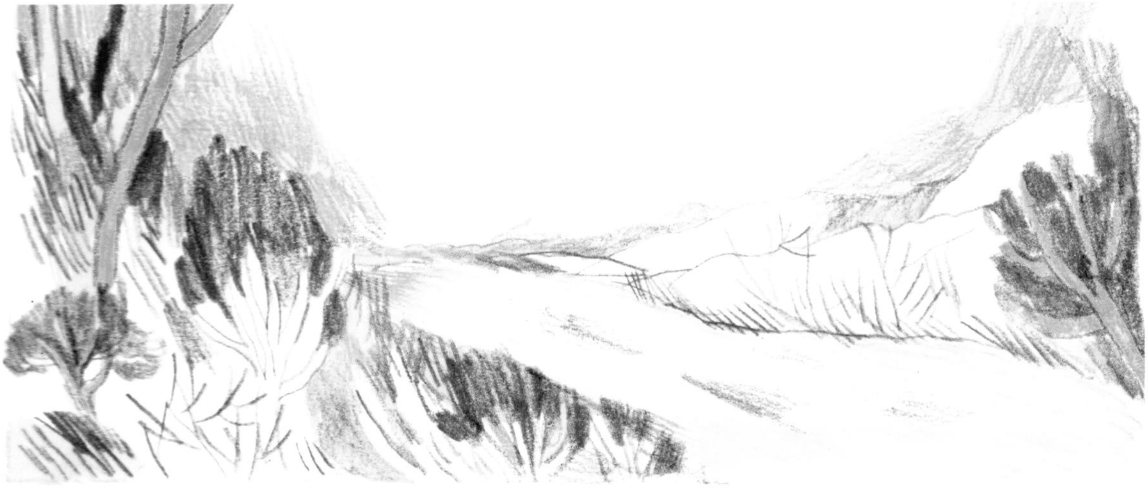

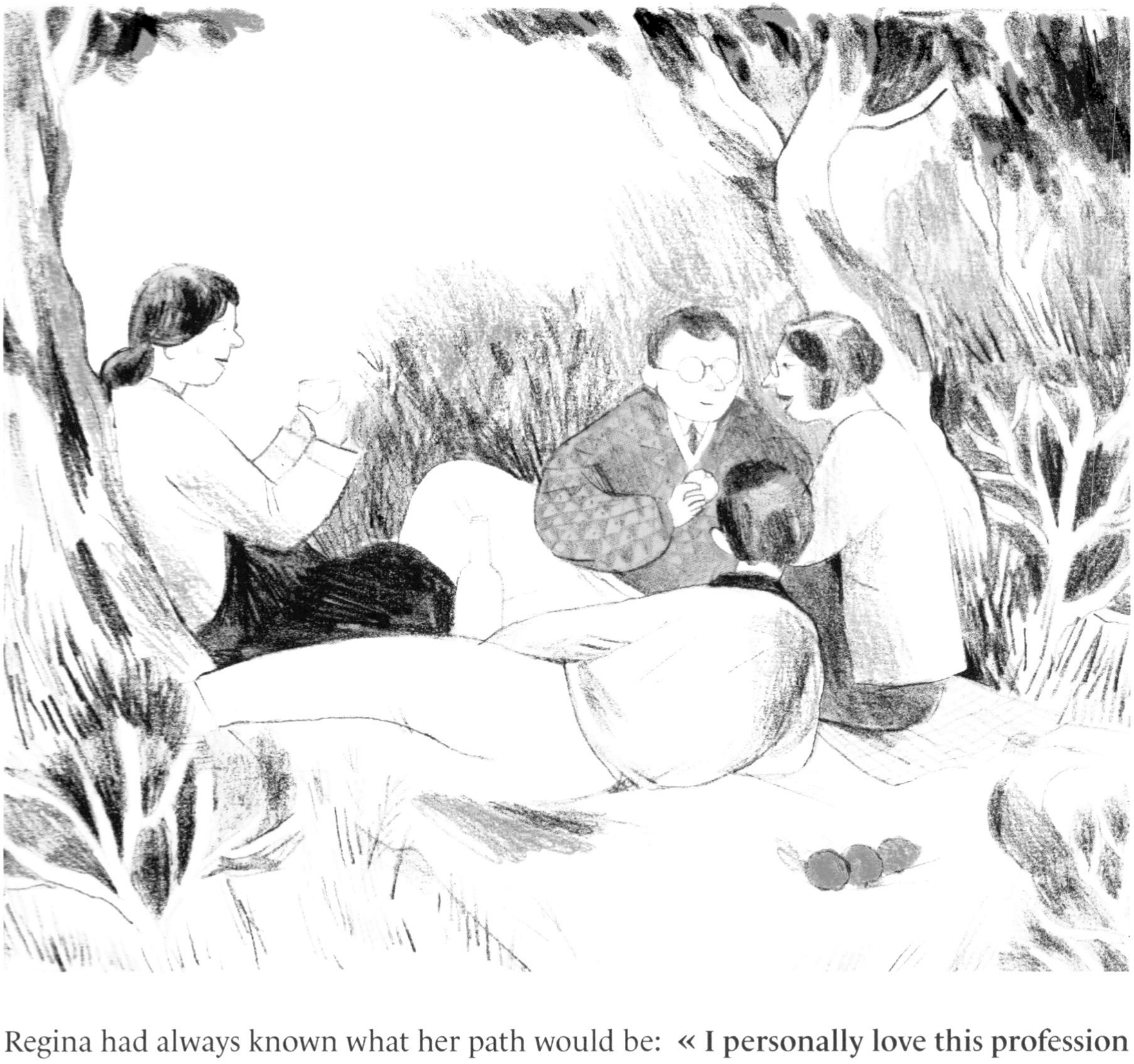

Regina had always known what her path would be: **« I personally love this profession and want very much to pursue it when that will be possible. »**

[*Can a Woman Hold Rabbinic Office?*, June 1930]

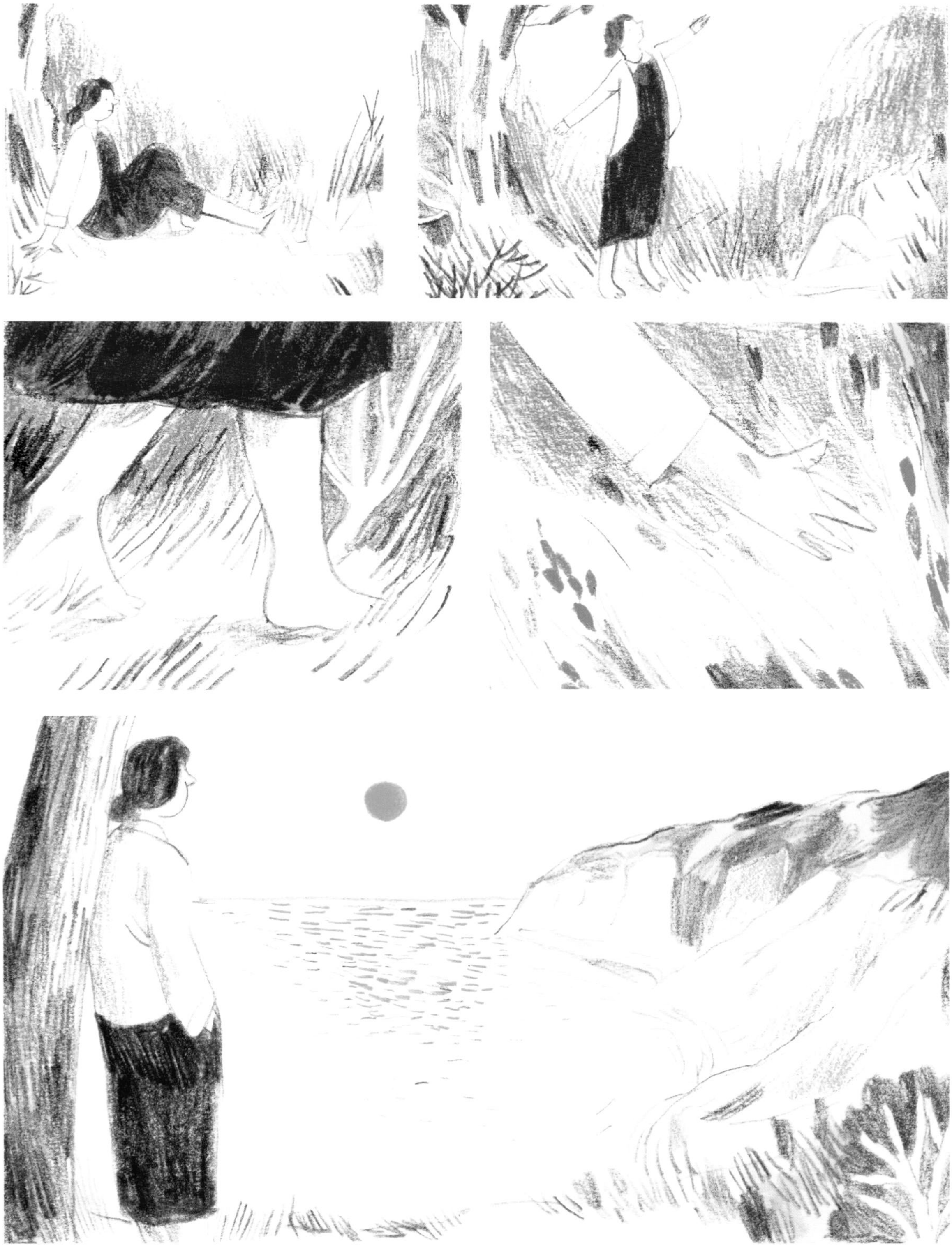

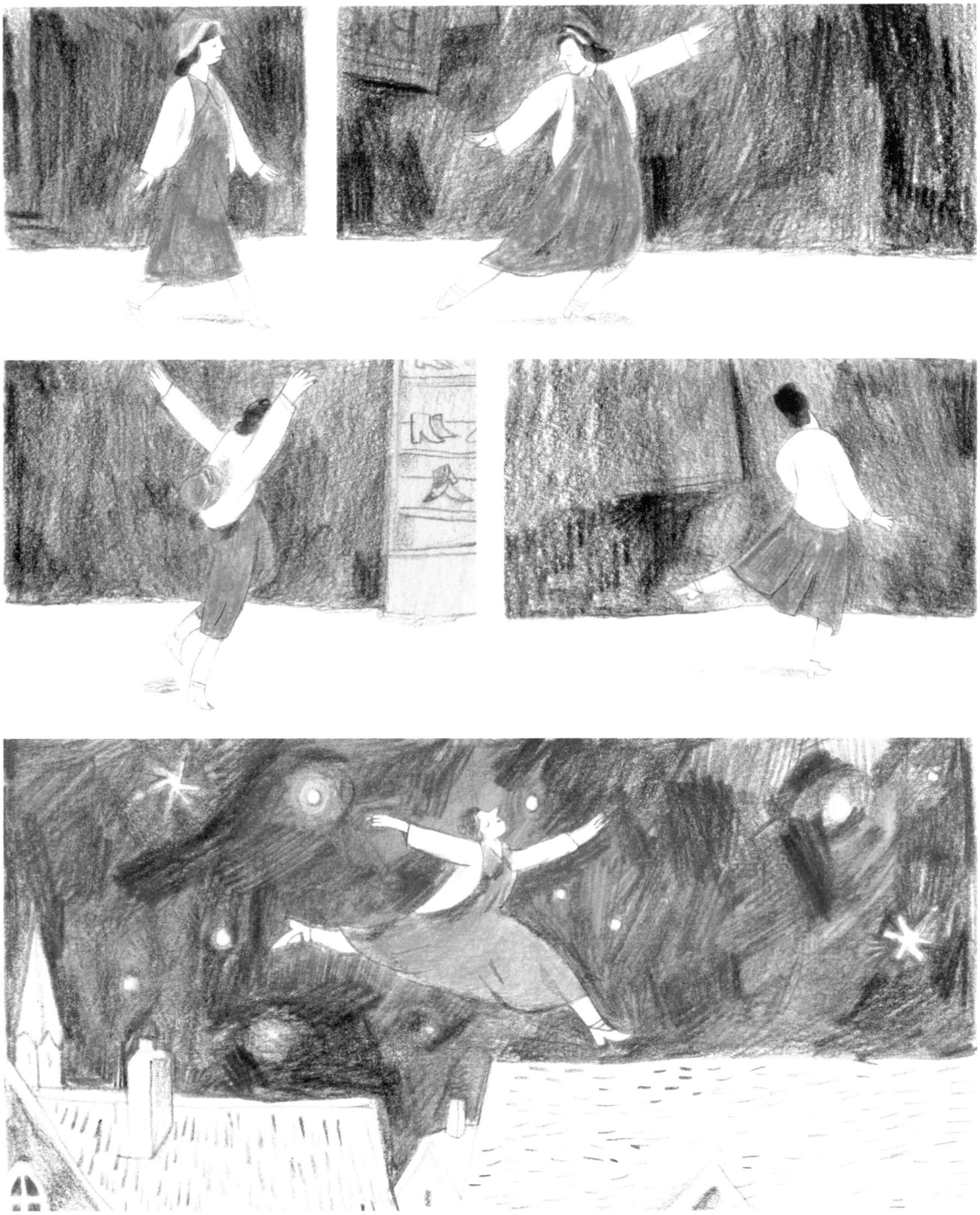

« Finally, it goes without saying, but it still must be firmly emphasized, that the only men and women who should devote themselves to the job of rabbi, teacher, and custodian of Jewish ideas, are those who are suffused with Jewish spirit, Jewish self-confidence, Jewish morality, purity and Jewish holiness, who could say, together with the prophet Jeremiah (20:9):

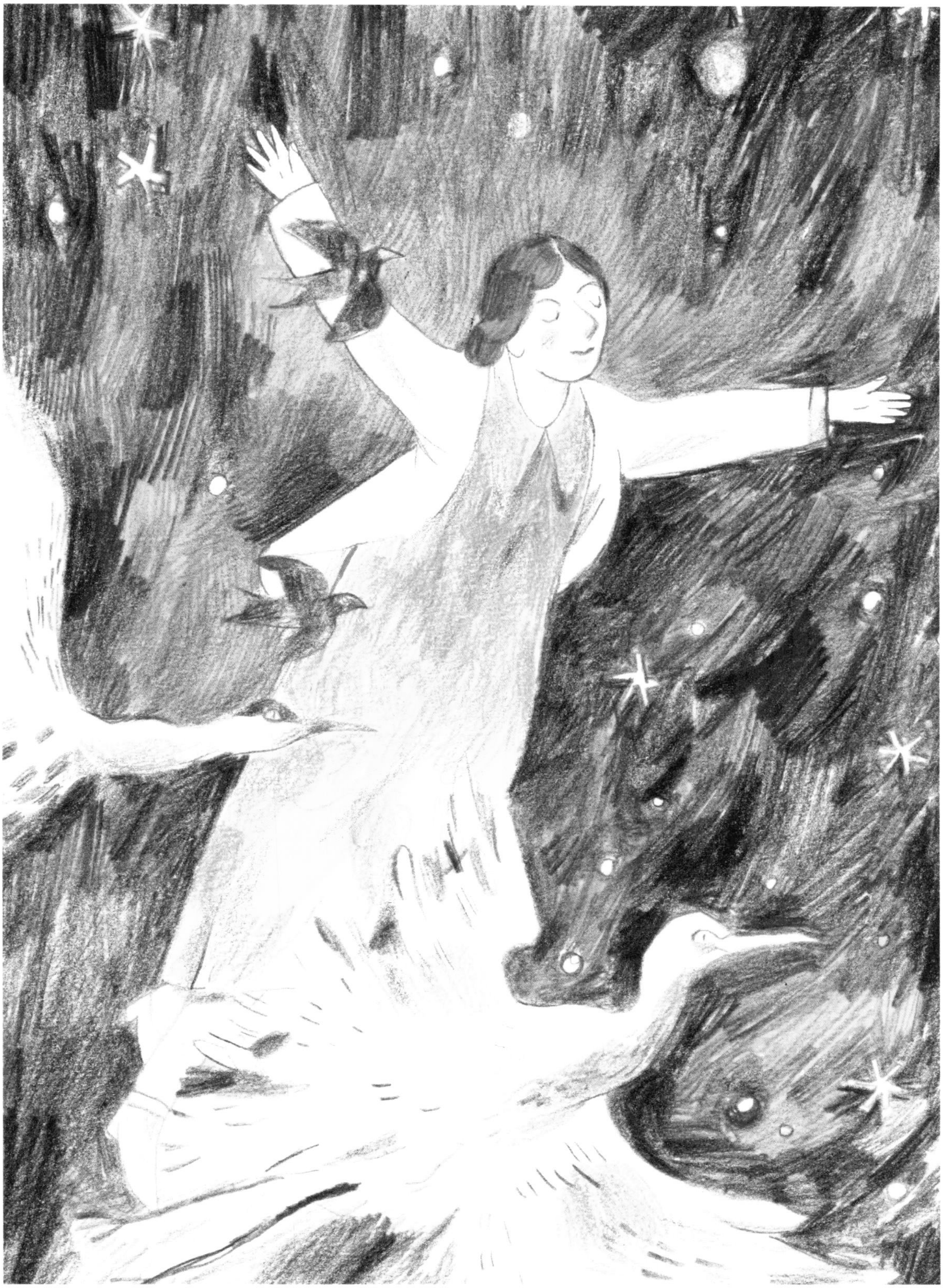

‘But His word was in my heart as a burning flame, shut up in my bones.’ I must fight for God. » [*Can a Woman Hold Rabbinic Office?*, June 1930]

18

Regina's ordination request was denied by the seminary faculty at the end of her studies.

And with Goodness and Mercy

1935 – 1944

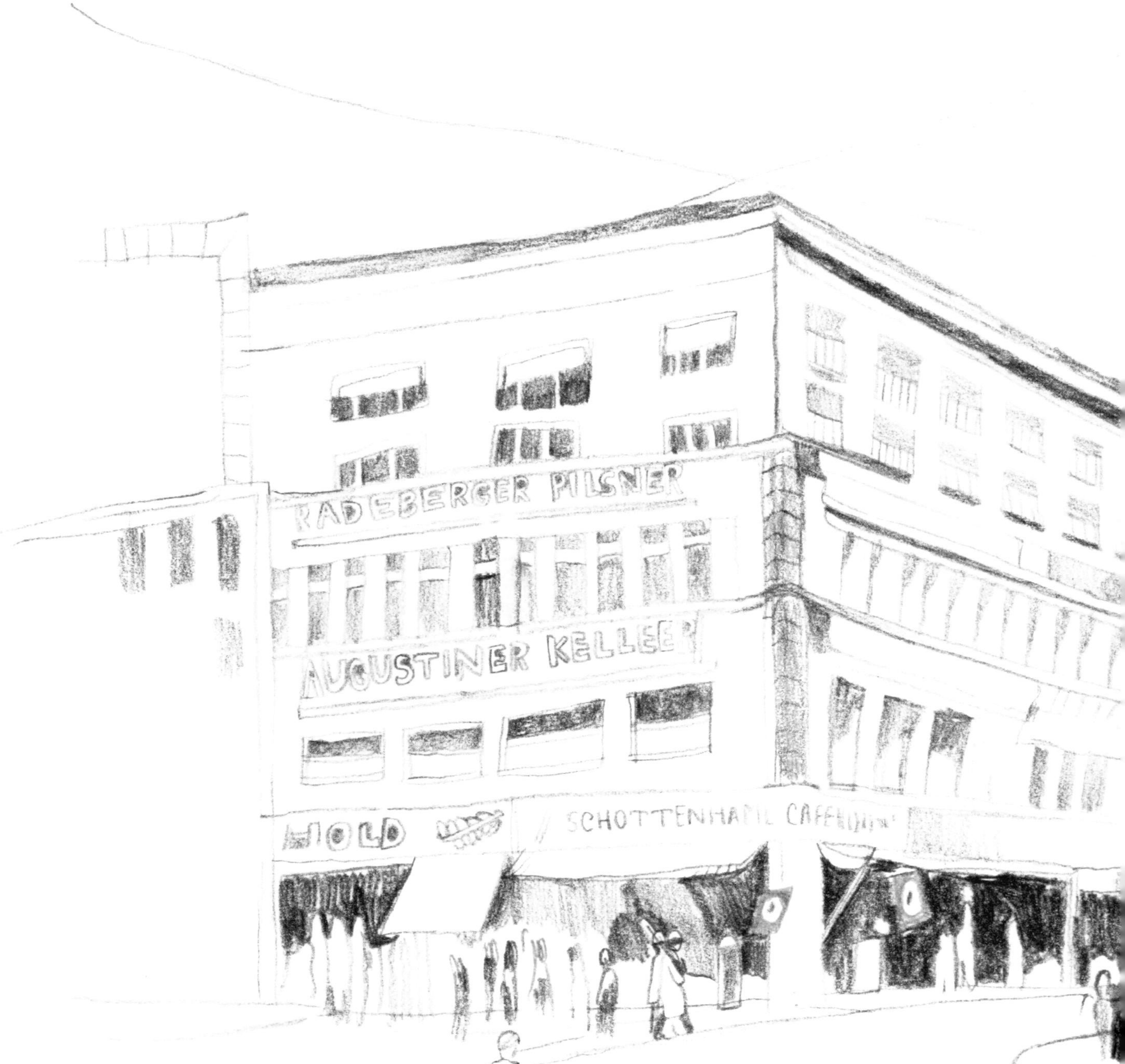
RADEBERGER PILSNER
AUGUSTINER KELLER
HOLD

Four years later, after Regina's persistent petitioning, the liberal rabbi Max Deineman tested her knowledge of various halachic subjects and granted her semikha in 1935. Still, it was unclear what title she should take, since "rabbiner" was a masculine noun, and referred to men, while the feminine version, "Frau Rabbinerin" (Mrs. Rabbi), was commonly used to refer to rabbis' wives. Instead, she became Fraulein Rabbinerin (Miss Rabbi) Regina Jonas. Regina held different positions in the Jewish community in Berlin and tried to gain a foothold as a rabbinical figure despite leadership's reluctance. During this time, the Nazis took control of the German government and passed the Nuremberg Laws, depriving Jews of basic civil rights. By the time the war began in 1939, many Jewish leaders had fled the country or been deported. The scarcity of rabbis, as well as the greater need for moral and practical support among German Jews, enabled Regina to take on more roles in the community than she might have been allowed in better times.

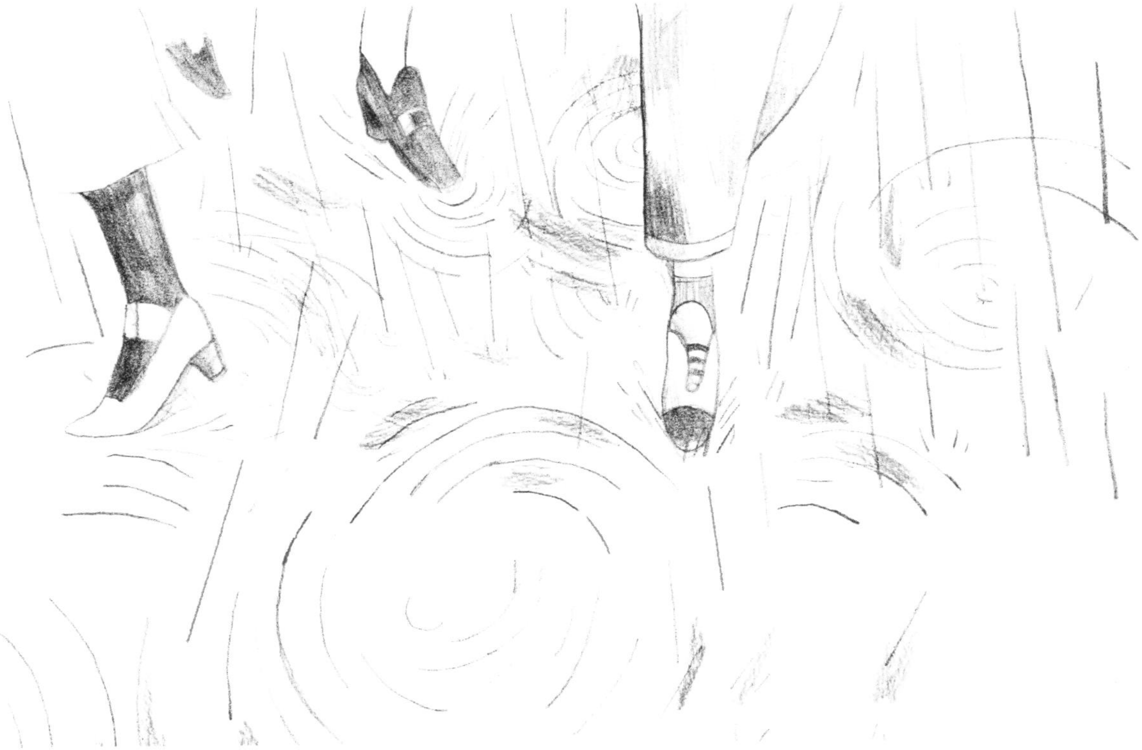

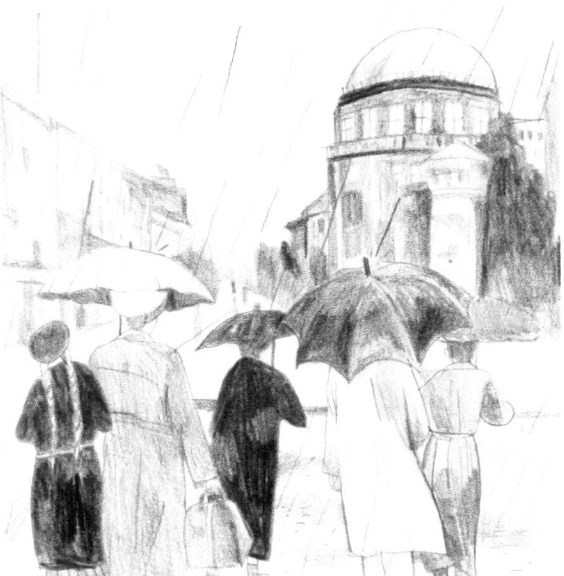

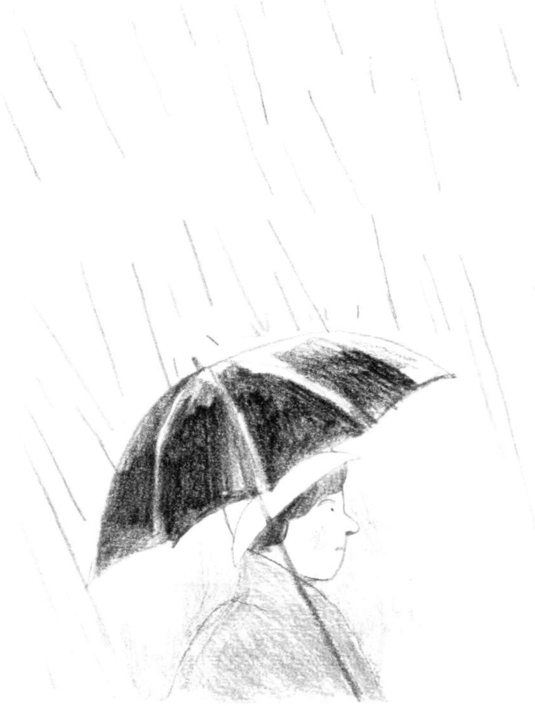

In the various positions she held throughout her career, Regina emphasized the pastoral care of the elderly, the infirm, and the disabled in the Jewish community. She acted as a spiritual guide and lectured in Jewish hospitals and nursing homes. She raised funds for charity, and collected food and clothing for the needy.

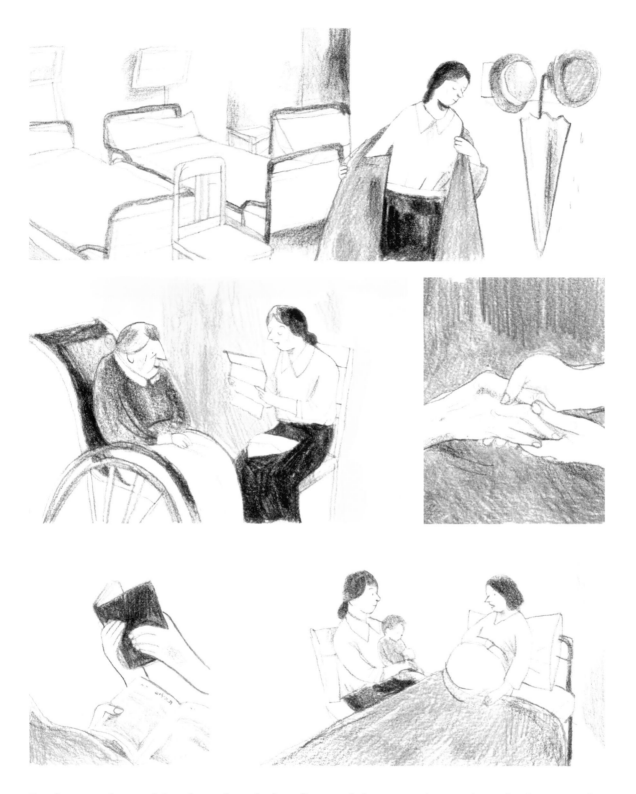

Regina saw her spiritual work as being first and foremost in service of others: « The solemn service of God is that of the neighbor, and the most sacred service is that performed for the most downtrodden, those struck by misfortune, the helpless, fearful, worried, the person who despairs of life. » [Interview given to *Jüdische Nachtrichtenblatt*, 1938]

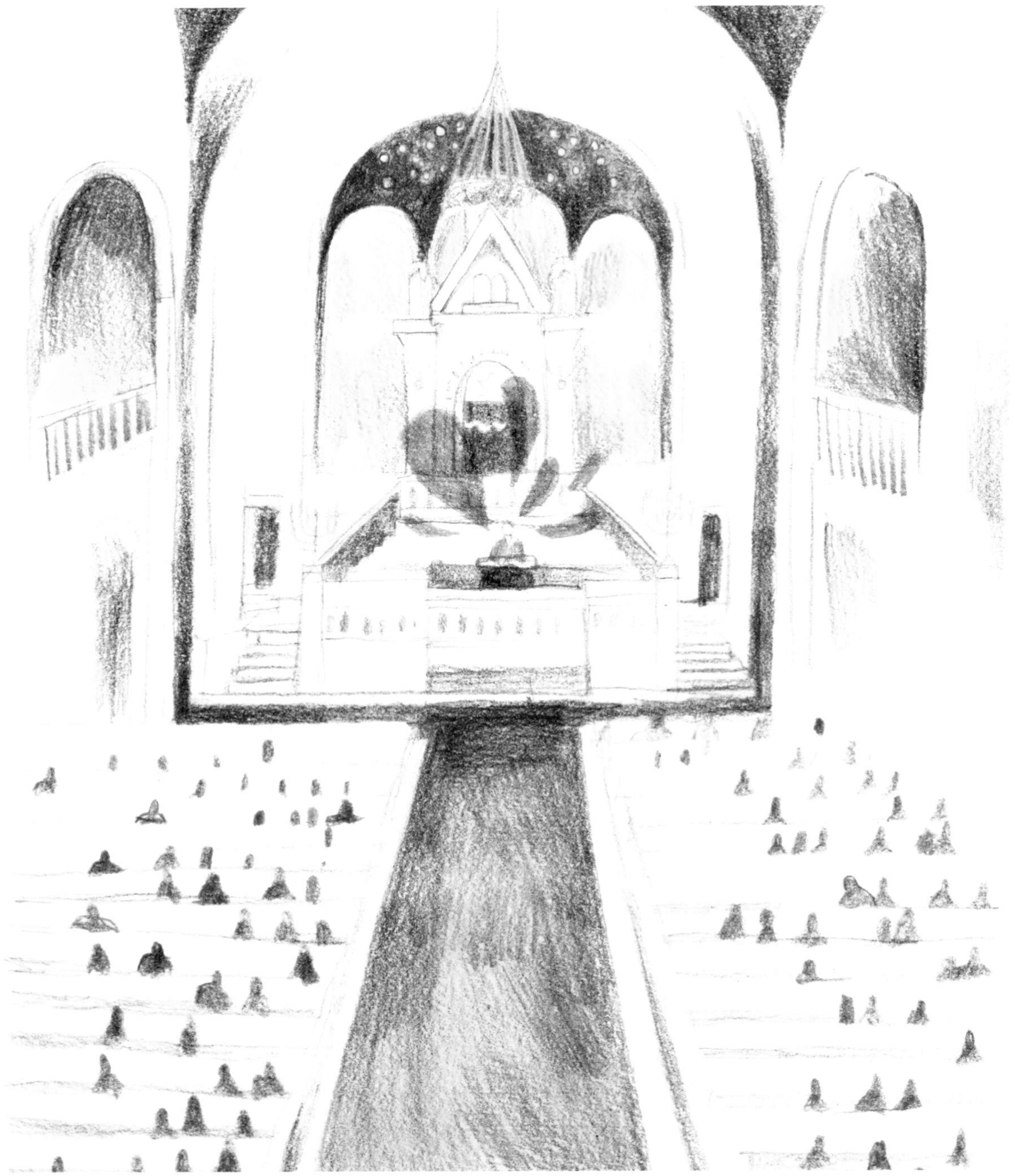

Her dream of being appointed to lead a community as a rabbi was never realized, but she traveled to various congregations across Germany where she gave guest sermons. Regina saved letters she received from congregants, which were later found among the documents she had taken care to hide before her deportation: **« In her sincere rabbinic motherly way [she] did me a great service, so that I don't know how I can ever thank her. It has now been proven to me that Jewish humanism is not an empty phrase but a reality, and I will contribute my part so that this magnanimous deed will not remain hidden. »**

« [She] knows how to handle broken and despairing hearts, to elevate them, and to inspire and excite them with the wealth of her learning. »

[Letters from congregations Regina visited]

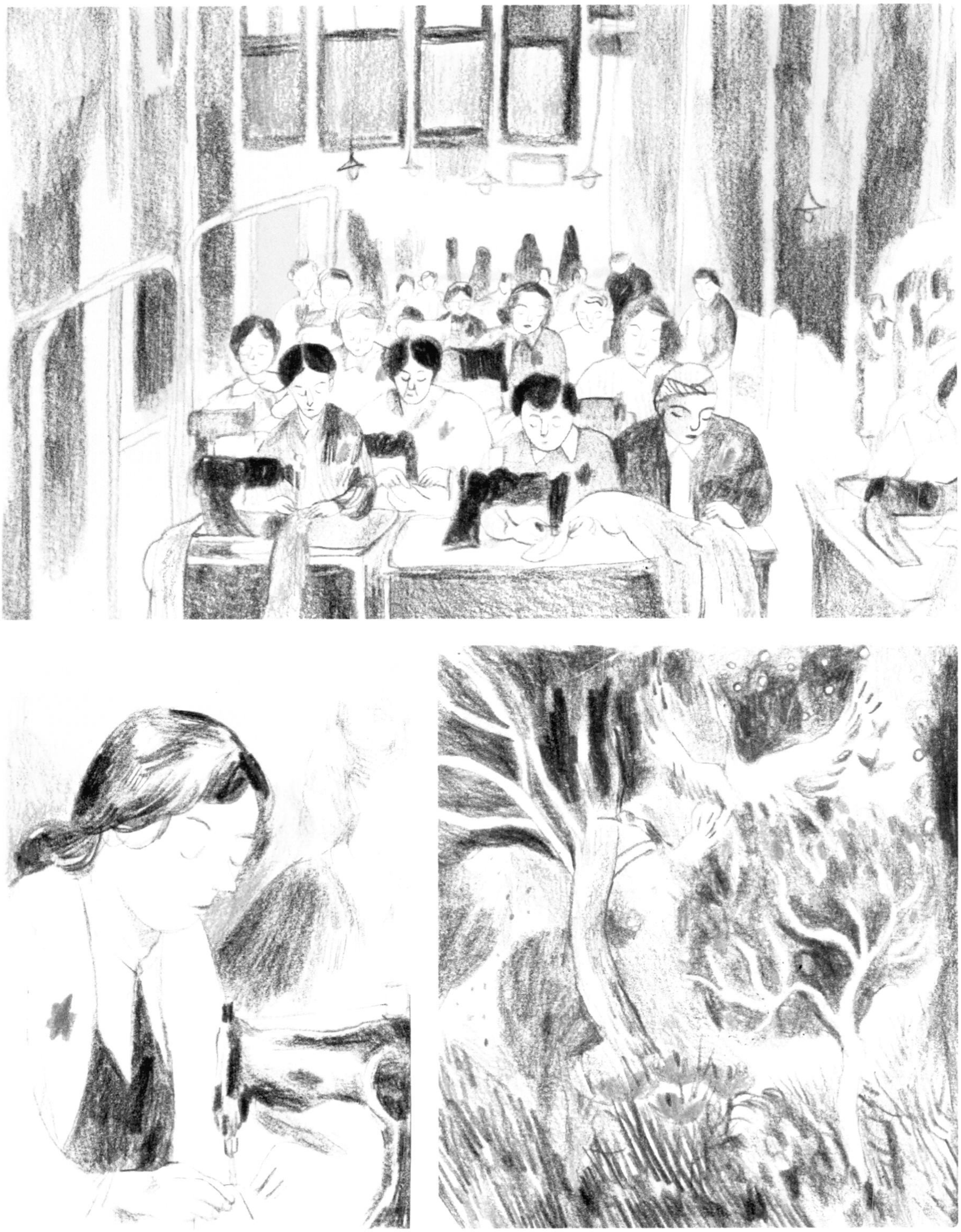

Recalling their time in Berlin during the war, one survivor remembered Regina's efforts and impact on the people: « **Where she lectured to the prisoners and forced laborers, they filled the room to bursting, and those who could not fit stood in the doorways until they spilled out into the street.** » [Survivor's testimony, Berlin]

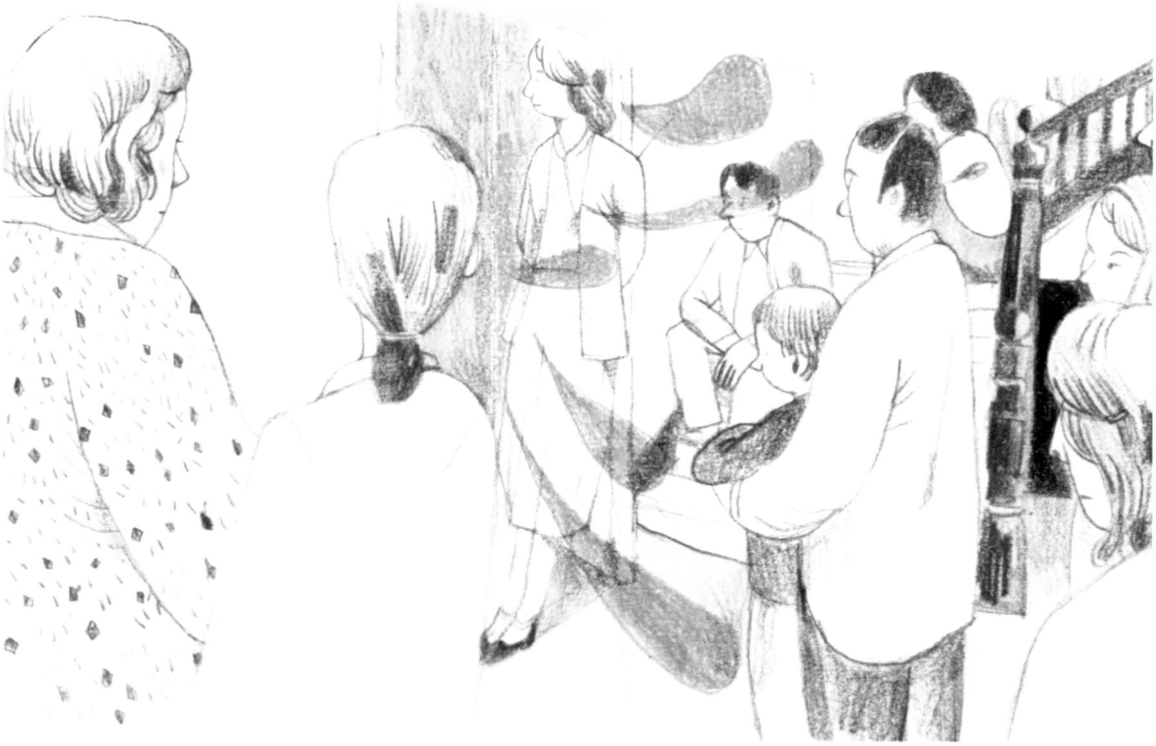

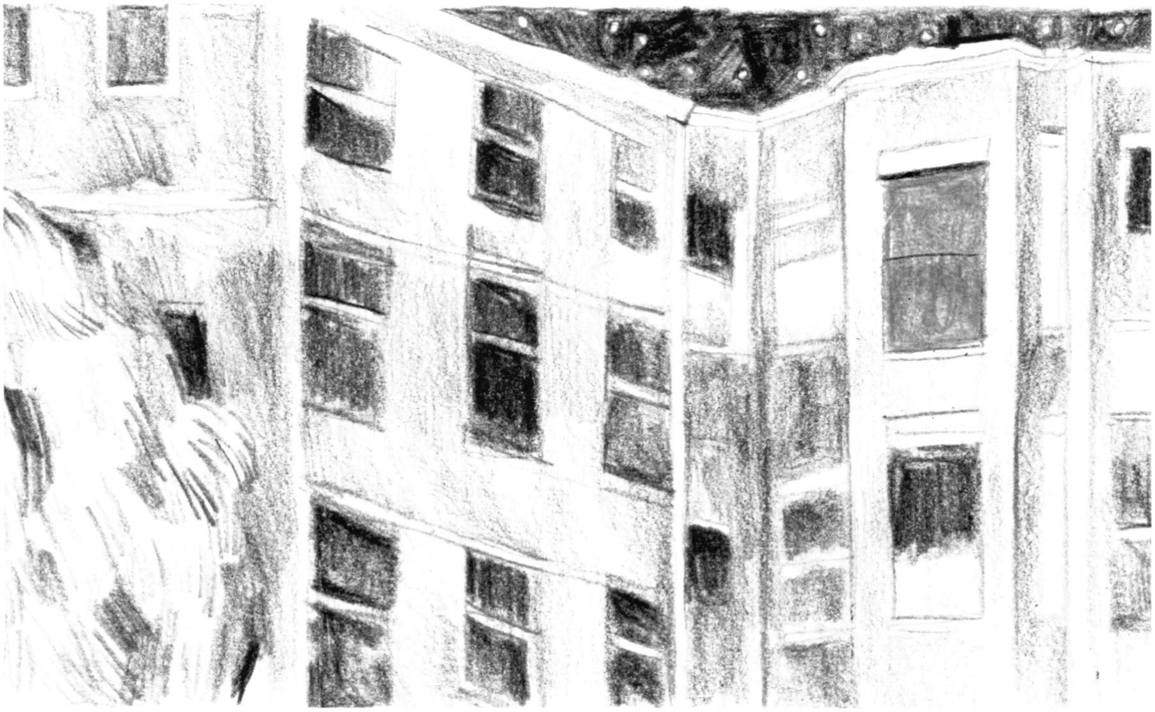

POST

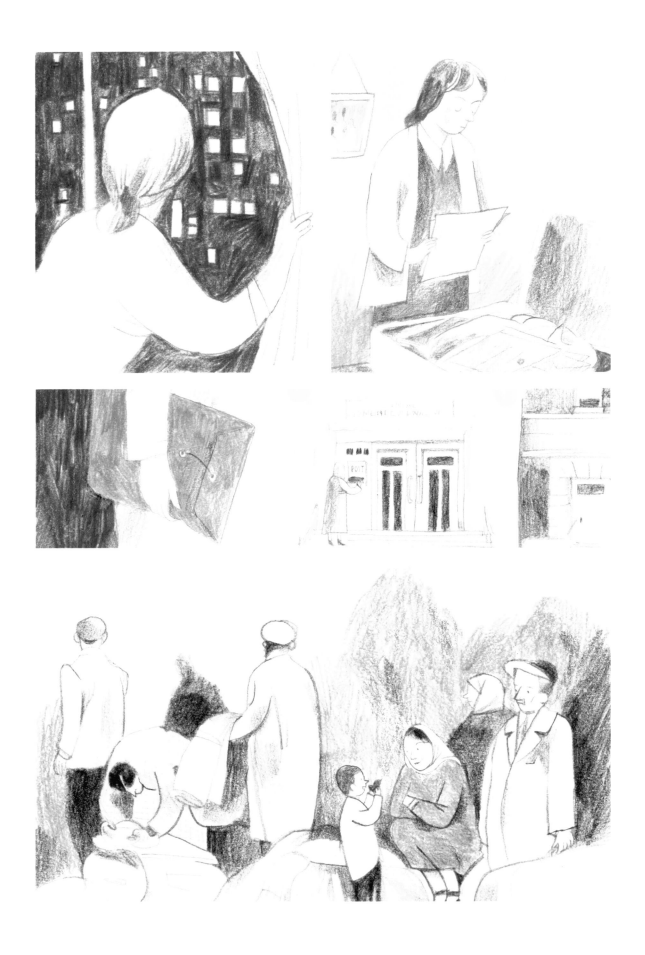

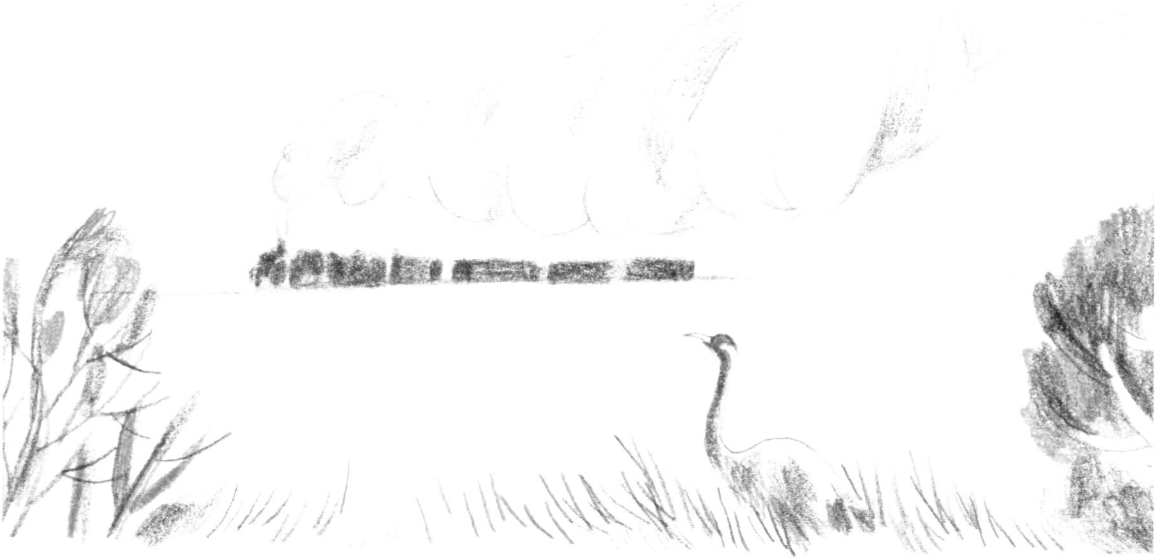

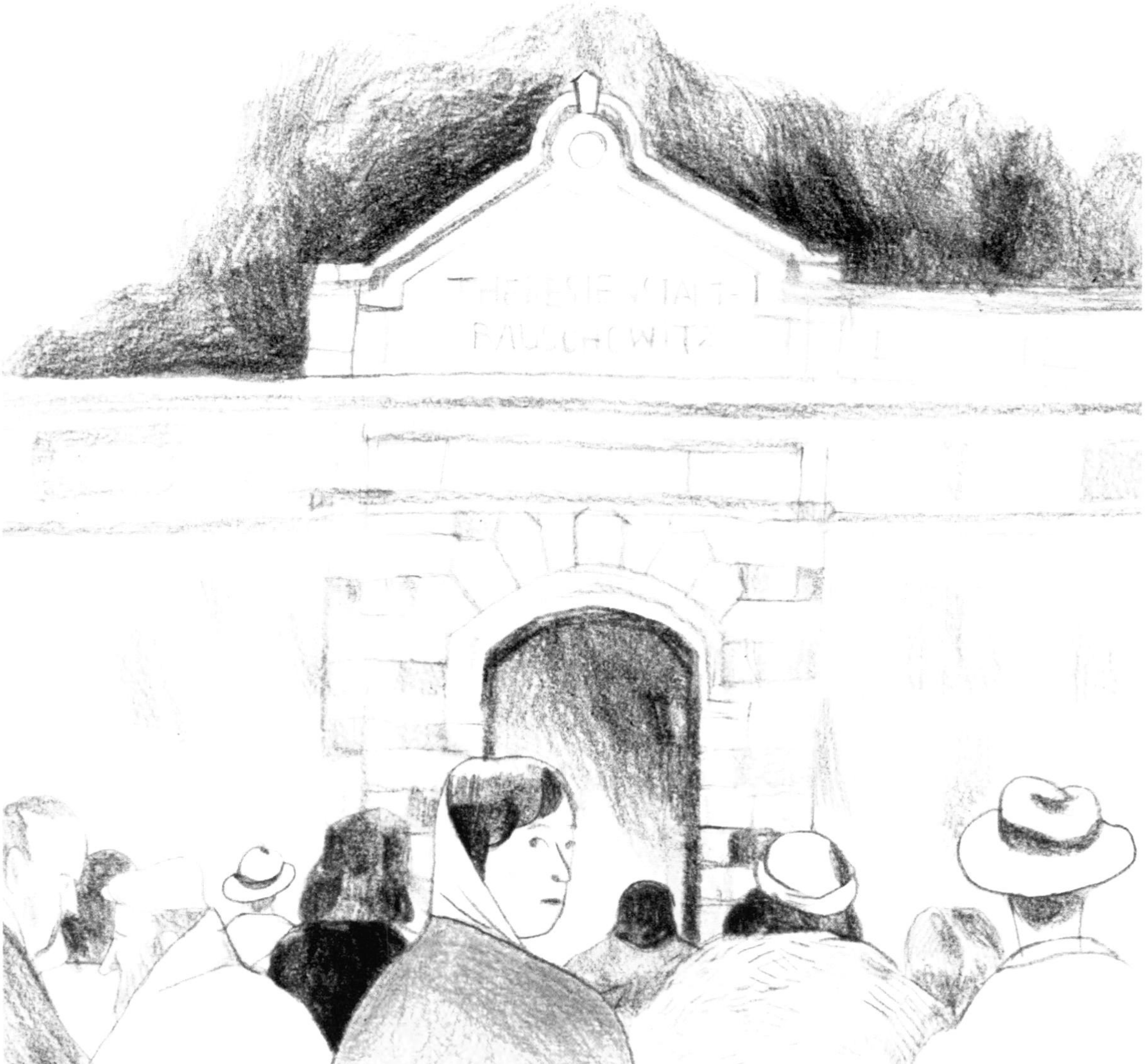

In 1942, Regina Jonas was deported with her mother to the Theresienstadt ghetto. While detained there, she volunteered in a mutual aid organization and helped new prisoners adjust to their startling and sudden circumstances. She gave lectures and sermons and helped to relieve some of her people's despair.

A handwritten list of twenty-four subjects on which Regina spoke was preserved in the Theresienstadt archive, titled *Lectures by the Only Female Rabbi: Regina Jonas.*

« Our Jewish people have been sent by God into history as a blessed nation. To be 'blessed by God' means, to give wherever one steps, in every life situation, blessings, kindness, faithfulness—humility before God, selfless and devoted love to His creatures, to sustain the world. To erect these fundamental pillars of the world was and is Israel's task.

Man and woman alike have taken on this task with the same Jewish devotion.

Towards this ideal our grave [and] trying work in Theresienstadt caters.... To be servants of God and as such to be transported from earthly into eternal spheres. May all our work be a blessing for Israel's future, and the future of humanity. »

[From a sermon given at Theresienstadt]

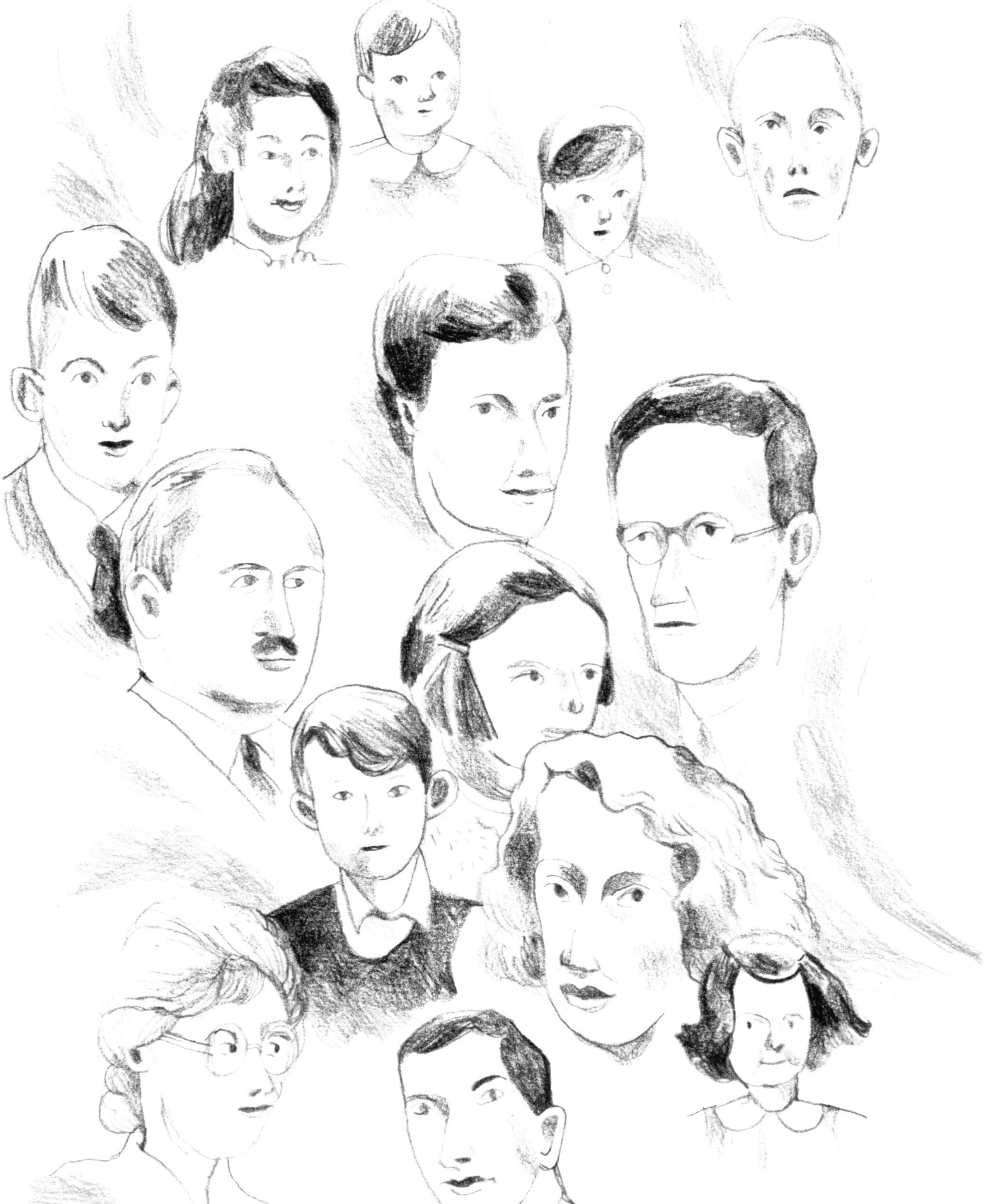

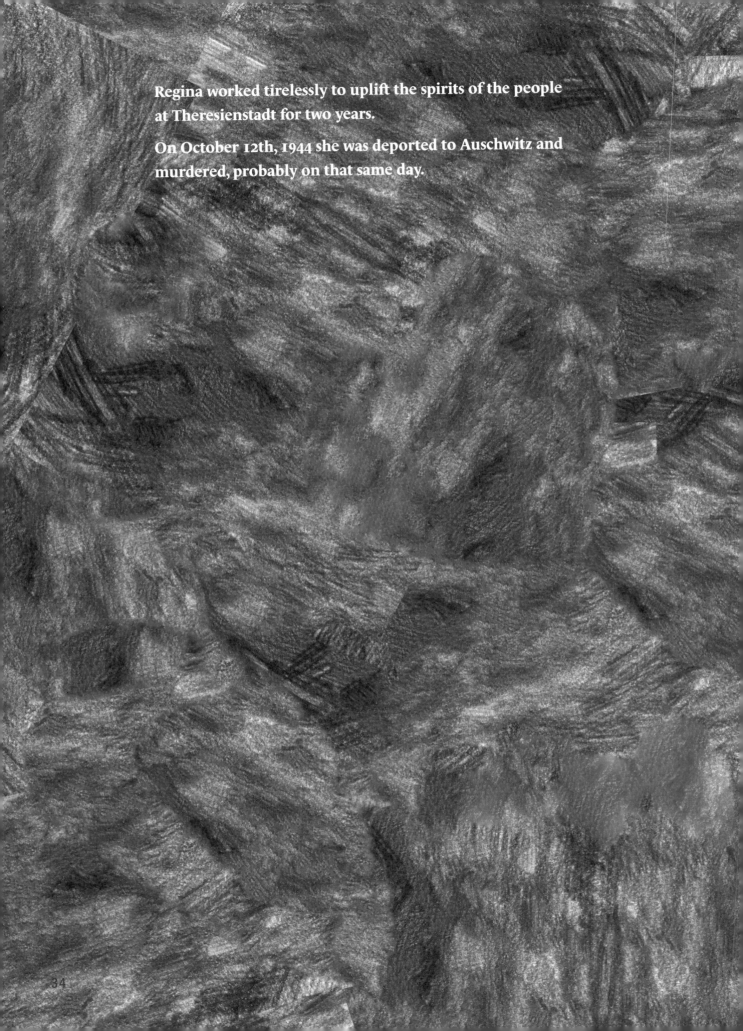

Regina worked tirelessly to uplift the spirits of the people at Theresienstadt for two years.

On October 12th, 1944 she was deported to Auschwitz and murdered, probably on that same day.

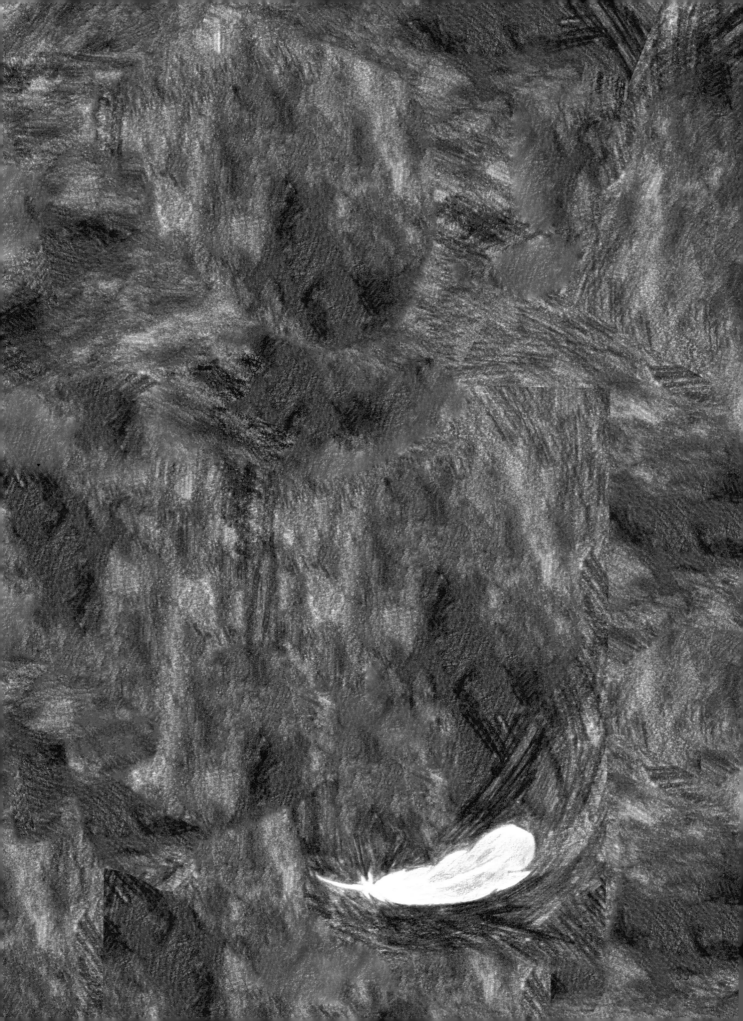

And You Will Know God

1996–

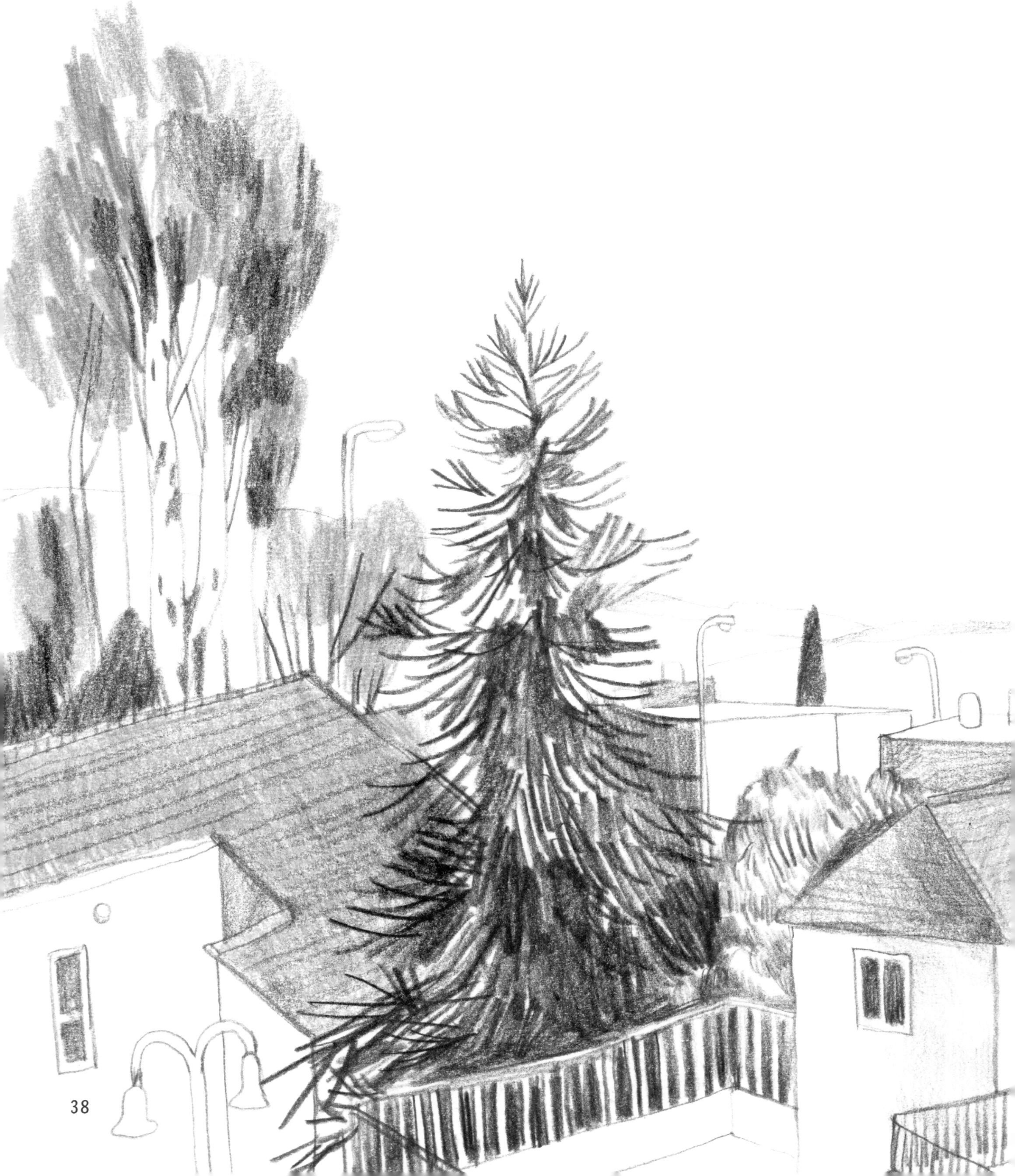

I was raised in a small community in Israel that liked to consider itself liberal, in an American immigrant family that threw around the term "feminism" pretty easily. My sister and I were expected to accompany my mother to the synagogue, as my brothers accompanied my father. There were no exceptions made for us when it came to most religious responsibilities—daily prayers, keeping the very detailed Shabbat laws. But there always seemed to be a mysterious wall around certain issues, where our participation didn't seem to count. Some unknown logic dictated that while the time had passed for some gendered restrictions—like women being barred from studying Torah—others were eternal, like women being barred from reading Torah to the congregation in a minyan. Compared to more restrictive communities, our religious practice exemplified the farthest reach of feminism within halachic Judaism. So this must be the best option, I figured. My unease didn't have a clear shape or words, just a nagging feeling that something was not quite right. That, despite all the explanations and reasoning, as a woman, I was only eighty percent Jewish, not a hundred.

In 2015, when I was eighteen years old, my younger brother had a tefillin ceremony for his bar mitzvah. It was held in a specific section of the Western Wall, where there is no partition, and all genders can be together.

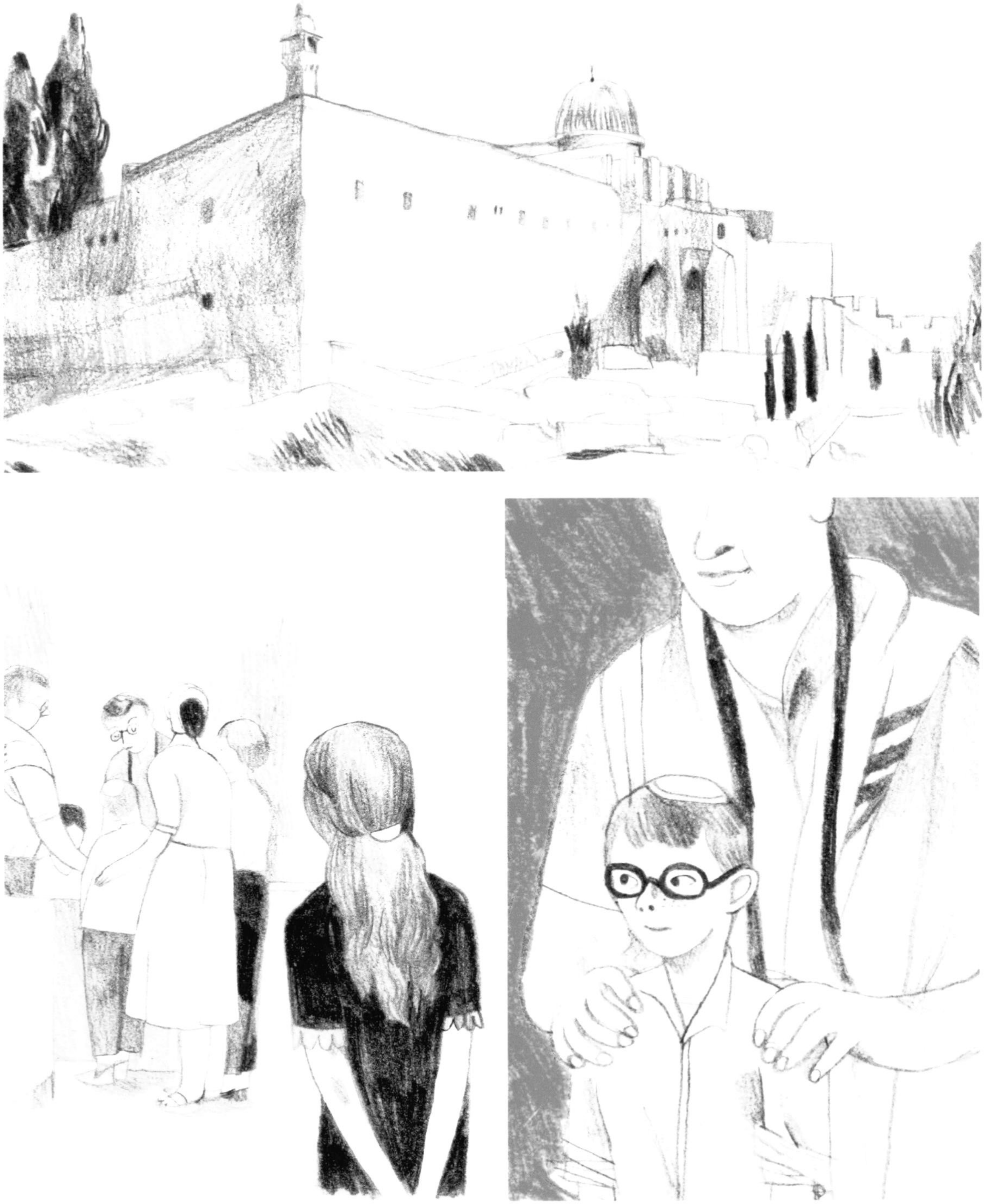

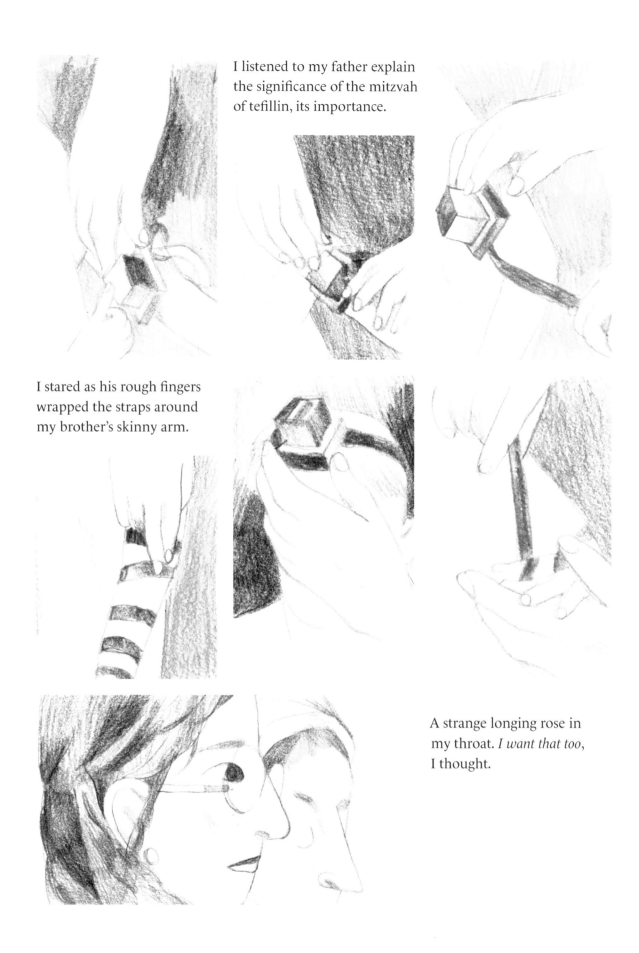

I listened to my father explain the significance of the mitzvah of tefillin, its importance.

I stared as his rough fingers wrapped the straps around my brother's skinny arm.

A strange longing rose in my throat. *I want that too*, I thought.

Three years later, I flew to New York to participate in a summer program in an egalitarian beit midrash, where women and men learn Torah together. I didn't know exactly what I was looking for, only that that same yearning still nagged at me.

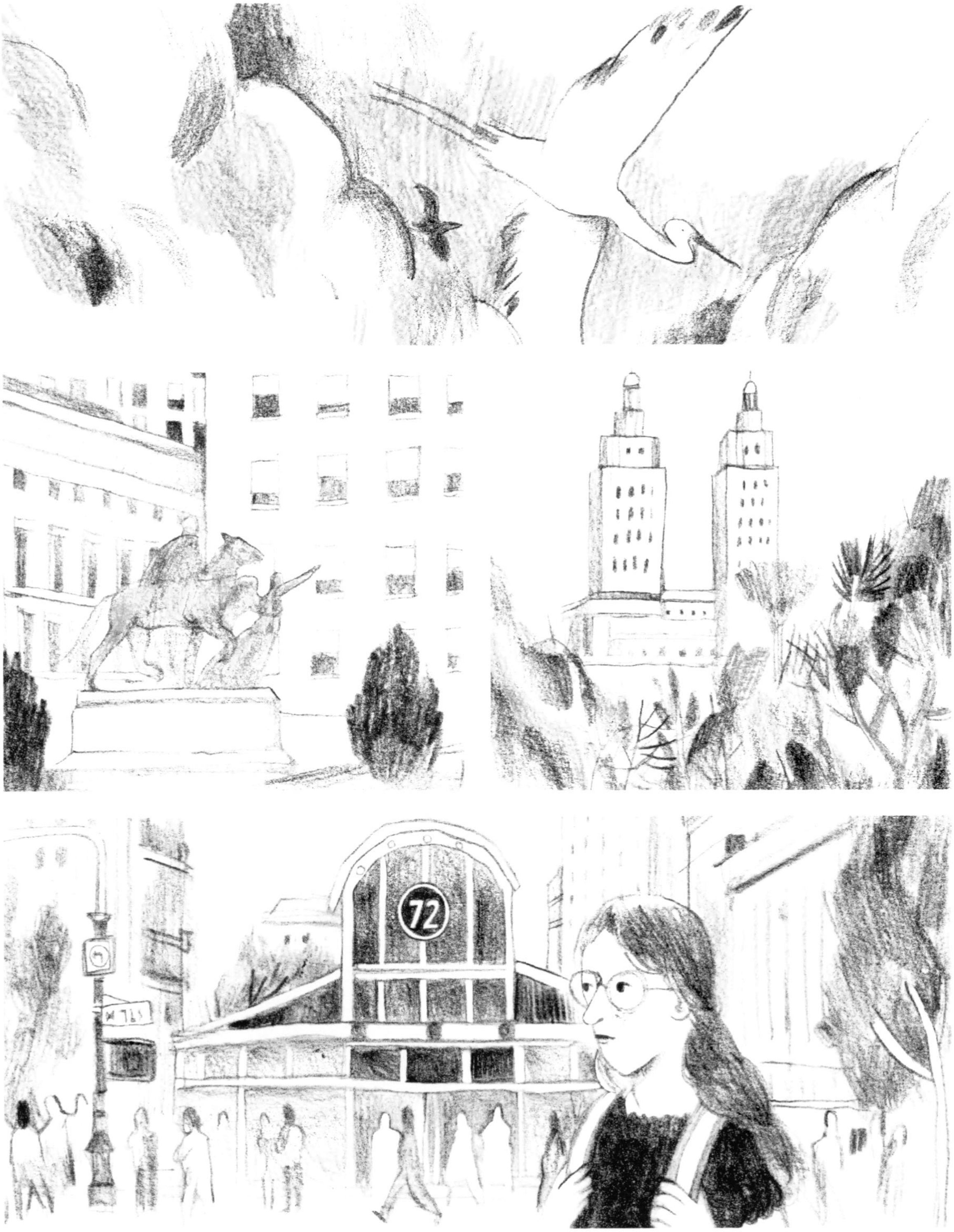
72

During the morning prayers on the first day, I looked around the room. The words were the same words I had always recited; the melodies were the same familiar melodies. But everything was so different. There was no partition. One of the female students led the service, wrapped in a tallis and tefillin.

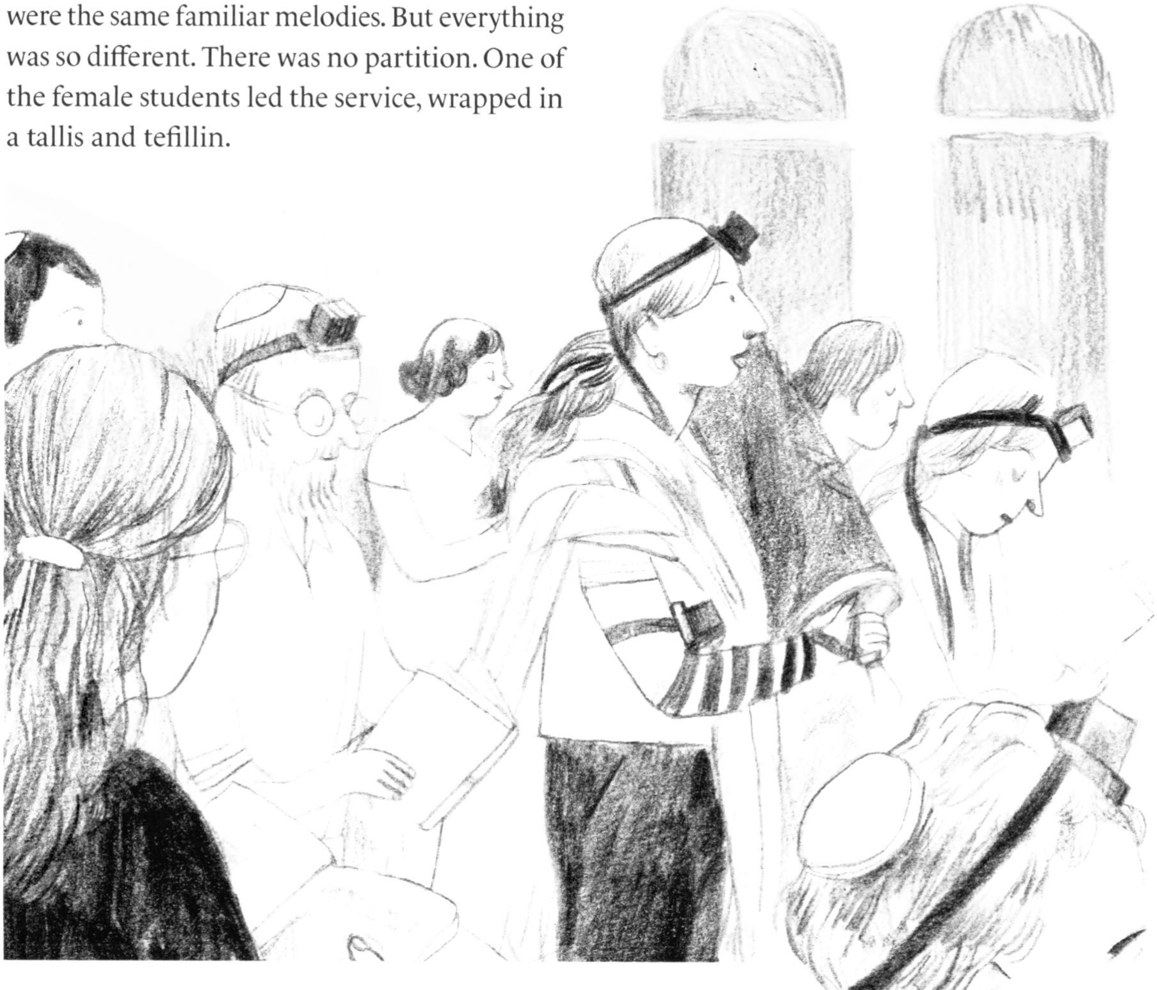

And afterwards one of the teachers, Rabbi Leah, stood up and gave a dvar torah. *Oh,* I thought, *this is how it can be.*

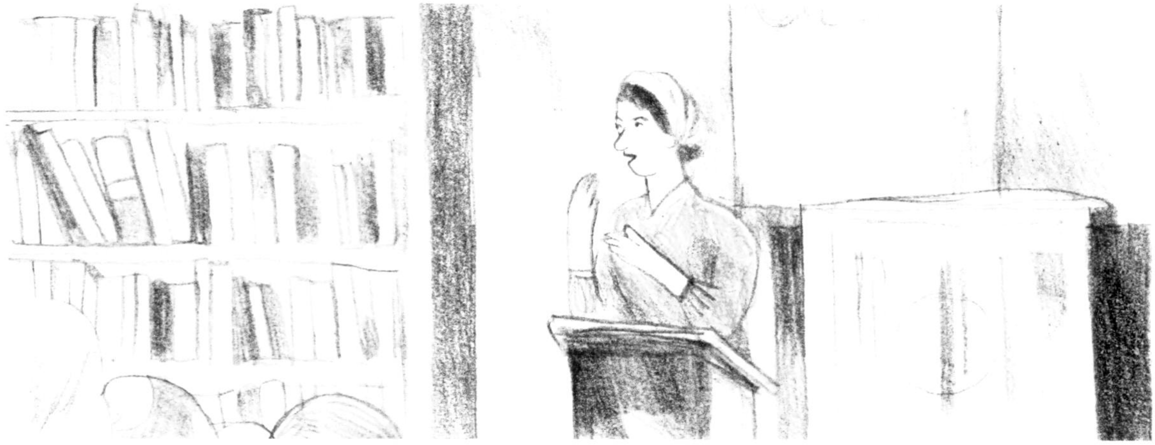

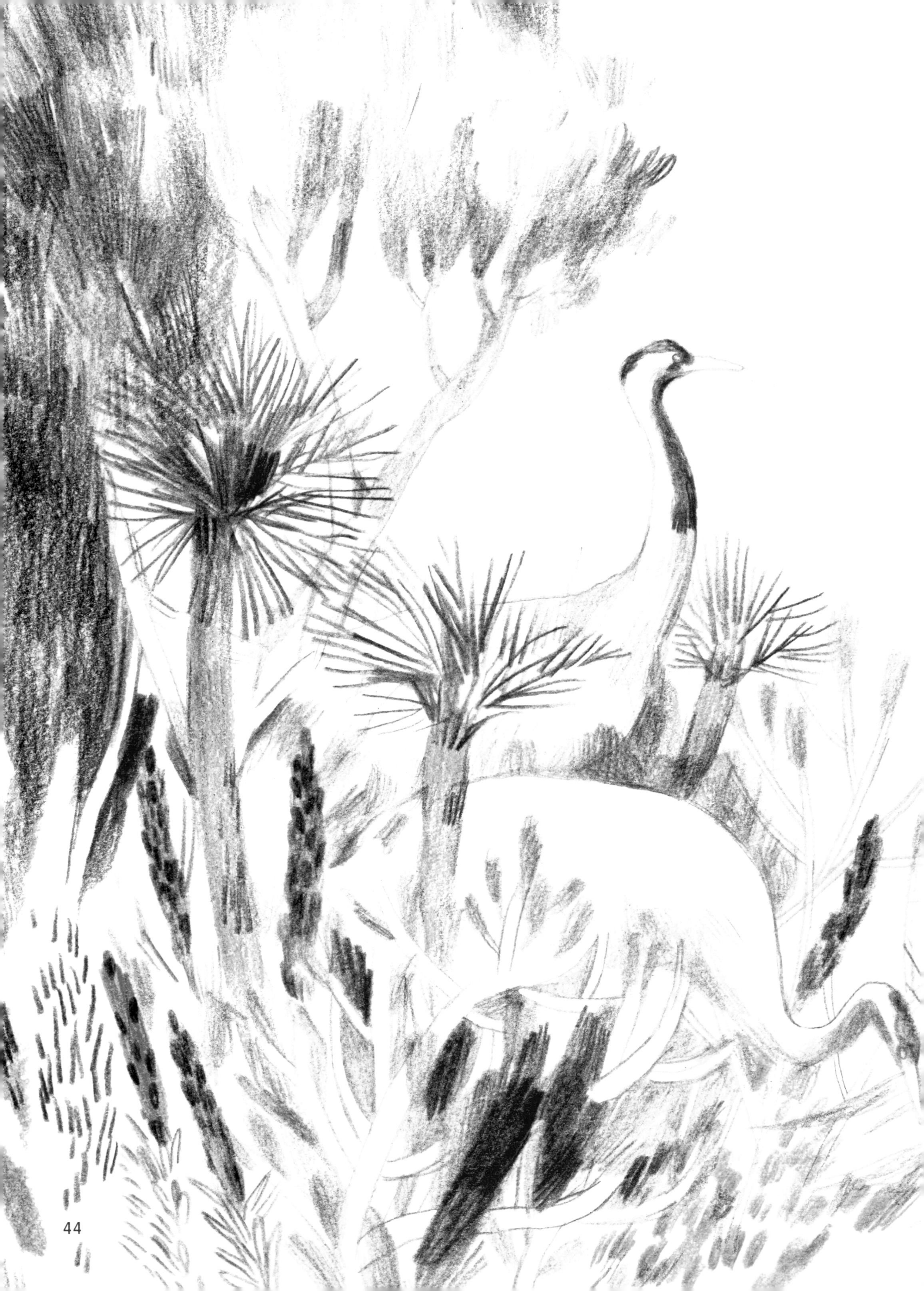

A few weeks after I got home,
I started wearing tefillin.

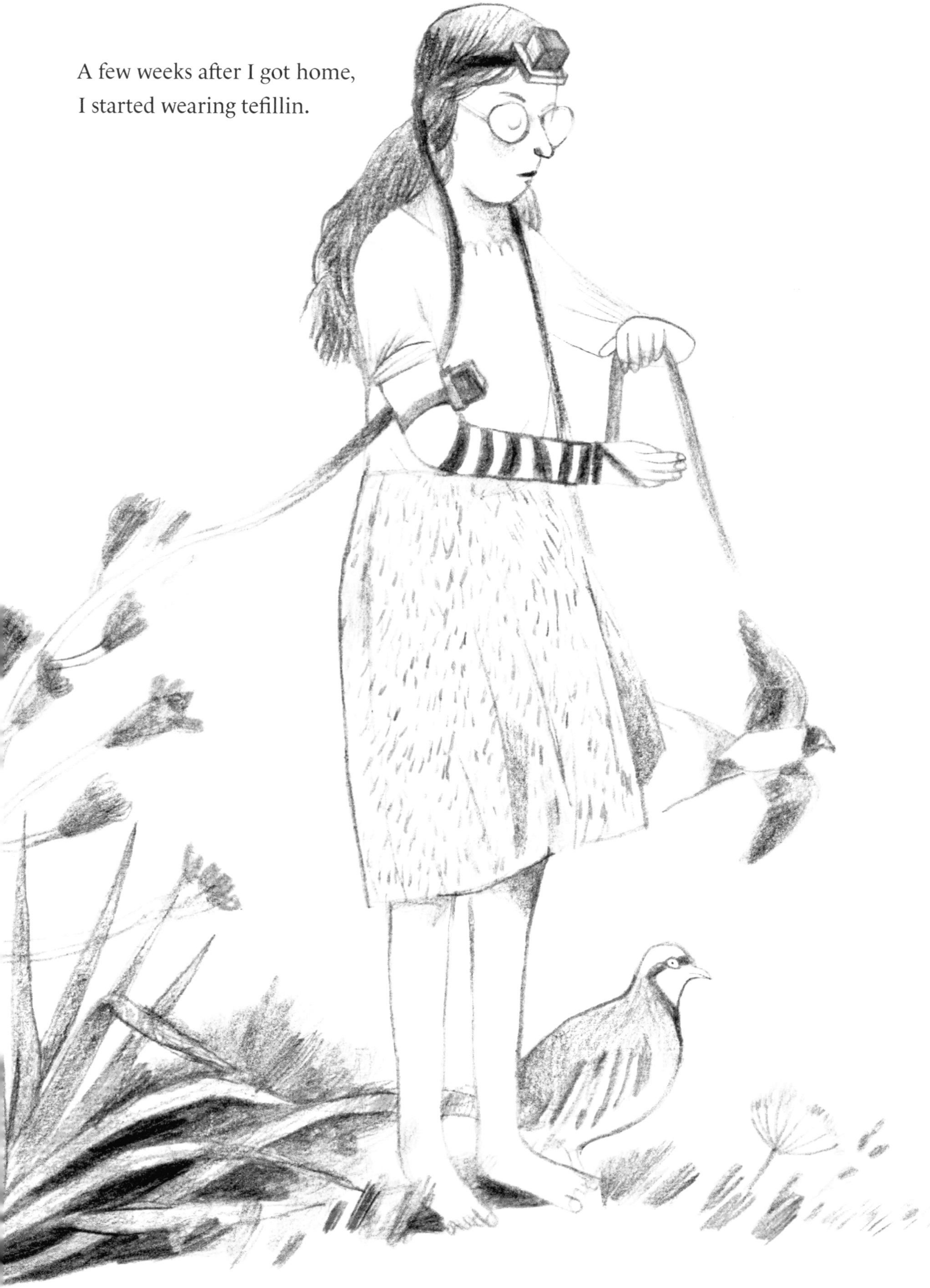

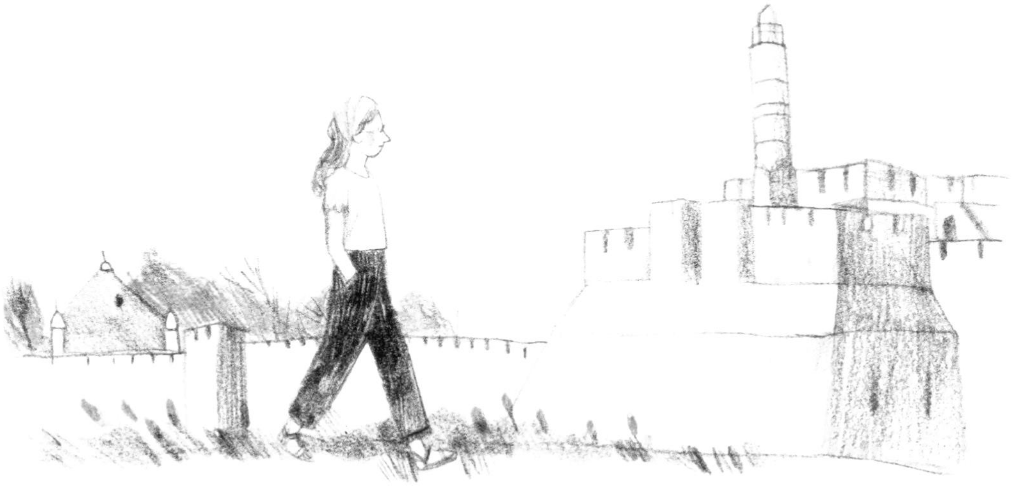

I never wanted to be a rabbi. But I did want to be more than I was told I could be. To feel more, to do more, to love more, to connect more. Not to hear "that's just how it is" anymore, or "women have a different role, and that's also important."

Regina was a fighter for justice. She wanted the world to be more equal, and for society to benefit from women's talents.

But I also know that what really motivated her was love. She loved Judaism, the Torah, the people, and her community. She wanted to do good, and she wanted to do more. Even before the Holocaust cut it short, Regina's life was not easy. Very few people stood by her in her struggle. Her abilities were disregarded, and she was belittled and shunned. She worked for many years with no recognition.

And I thank her for that.

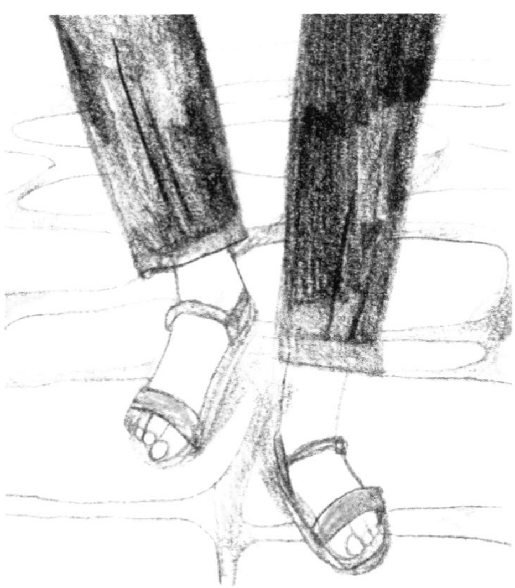

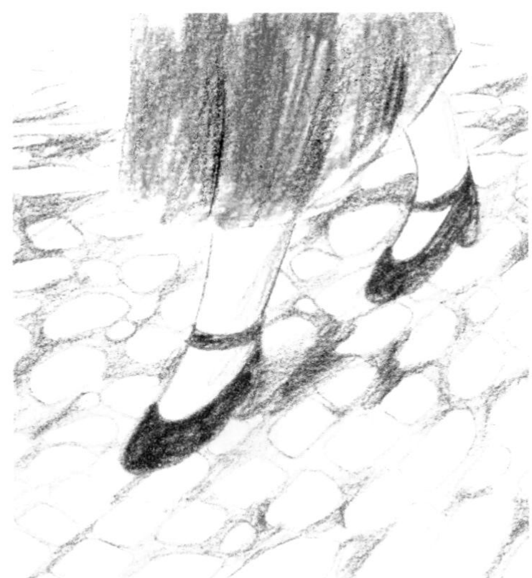

« I hope a time will come for all of us in which there will be no more questions on the subject of 'woman': for as long as there are questions, something is wrong. But if I must say what drove me as a woman to become a rabbi, two elements come to mind: my belief in the godly calling and my love for people.

God has placed abilities and callings in our hearts, without regard to gender. Thus each of us has the duty, whether man or woman, to realize those gifts God has given. If you look at things this way, one takes woman and man for what they are: human beings. »

[From an interview given to *Central-Verein Zeitung*, 1938]

After her death, Regina Jonas's story was forgotten.

Her name was mentioned infrequently in survivors' testimonies and academic papers. Leo Baeck and Victor Frankl, two giants of Jewish theology who survived the Holocaust, did not mention her in their writings on the topic. They knew Regina personally, but the figure of the first female rabbi did not appear in their accounts of the Theresienstadt ghetto.

In 1991, Dr. Katharina von Kellenbach, a professor of religious studies at St. Mary's College of Maryland, traveled to Germany to research the attitudes of the Jewish and Protestant establishments towards women who pursued ordination. In an archive in East Germany that was opened to visitors for the first time after the fall of the Iron Curtain, Dr. von Kellenbach found the envelope Regina had left at the Jewish community in Berlin before her deportation. It contained two photographs of her, her thesis, her semikha and teaching certificates, the letters she had received during that time, and other personal documents. This revelation, and the papers written by von Kellenbach in the wake of it, led to a posthumous recognition, rediscovery, and commemoration of Regina Jonas.

In the intervening years, many more women have been ordained as Rabbis. The first was Rabbi Sally Jane Preisand of the American Reform movement in 1972. However, Regina wasn't Reform or Conservative; she would have been "Orthodox" by today's standards, although no Orthodox Rabbis of her time recognized her authority.

As of this writing, over 1,200 women have been ordained as rabbis in the Orthodox, Reform, Conservative, and Reconstructionist movements, in Israel and around the world.

Glossary of Terms

beit din a Jewish court of law.

beit midrash literally "house of study," a room, institution, or educational program dedicated to the study of Jewish texts.

dvar torah a short sermon.

halacha Jewish law derived from biblical commandments, rabbinical decrees, and accepted customs.

lulav a palm branch. This is carried and shaken on the festival of Sukkot along with willow and myrtle branches and a citron fruit. Traditionally only men are required to perform this ritual.

minyan traditionally, a quorum of ten men required to recite certain prayers and read (chant) from the Torah.

rebbetzin, rabbanit an honorific title for rabbi's wives in Yiddish and Hebrew (respectively); in German, rabbinerin.

pasken to rule on a question of halacha.

tallis / tallit a fringed prayer shawl worn during morning services, traditionally by men.

tefillin phylacteries, traditionally worn by men.

Bibliography

Aryeh Dayan, "A Forgotten Myth," *Haaretz*, May 25, 2004.

Liz Elsby, "'I Shall Be What I Shall Be'—The Story of Rabbiner Regina Jonas," Yad Vashem, accessed June 5, 2023.

Elisa Klapheck, "Regina Jonas: August 3, 1902–1944," *The Shalvi/Hyman Encyclopedia of Jewish Women* (Jewish Women's Archive), last modified December 31, 1999.

Katharina von Kellenbach, "Denial and Defiance in the Work of Rabbi Regina Jonas," in *God's Name: Genocide and Religion in the Twentieth Century*, eds. Omer Bartov and Phyllis Mack (New York: Berghahn Books, 2010), 243–258.

Katharina von Kellenbach, "'God Does Not Oppress Any Human Being': The Life and Thought of Rabbi Regina Jonas," *The Leo Baeck Institute Year Book* 39, no. 1 (January 1994): 213–225.

Laura Major, "'Without Regard to Gender': A Halachic Treatise by the First Woman Rabbi," *Havruta* (Summer 2010): 78–84.

Tara Metal, "Excerpts from the Writings of Regina Jonas," *Jewish Women's Archive*, September 29, 2014.

Acknowledgments

Translations of Rabbi Jonas's writings courtesy of Rabbi Elisa Klapheck, Toby Axelrod, and Dr. Katharina Von Kellenbach.

Thank you to the Visual Communications department at Bezalel Academy of Art and Design, Jerusalem, and especially to my advisor Amit Trainin, my classmates, and dear friends.

somewhere

Somewhere is an imprint of Ayin Press that publishes kids' books, artist books, comics, zines, graphic novels, and illustrated works.

AYIN PRESS

Ayin Press is an artist-run publishing platform and production studio rooted in Jewish culture and emanating outward.